HADRIAN'S W

David J Breeze, BA, PhD, FSA

Hadrian's Wall is a complex monument, 73 miles long, but with additional frontier works to the west and east, outpost forts to the north and hinterland forts behind. This guidebook seeks to explain the background to the construction of the Wall, and offers a description of the various elements of the frontier, examining how it was built, and its function and describing the lives of the soldiers based on the Wall. This revised and updated second edition includes new information panels on Roman forts, granaries and bath houses; Roman religion; Hadrian; early archaeologists of the Wall; and the new national trail.

The second part of the book consists of a series of descriptions and tours of those sections of the Wall open to the public. While the core of the guidebook is formed by those elements of the frontier in the care of English Heritage, other sites are described, including South Shields, Wallsend, Vindolanda, Birdoswald and Maryport.

MUSEUM OF ANTIQUITIES, NEWCASTLE

A coin of the Emperor Hadrian
found in the River Tyne at Newcastle

WHAT IS HADRIAN'S WALL?

BELOW: Diagrammatic section across Hadrian's Wall. The Vallum was generally about 60 to 100 yards behind the Wall

BOTTOM: Reconstruction by Peter Connolly of Hadrian's Wall, showing a turret in the foreground and a milecastle beyond

BELOW RIGHT: A model of a stone milecastle in the Museum of Antiquities, Newcastle. There are gates to the north and south, to allow soldiers and civilians to pass through the Wall. A barrack block accommodated eight soldiers

BOTTOM RIGHT: A model of the fort at Benwell in the Museum of Antiquities, Newcastle. The fort lies astride the Wall, with three of its four main gates opening north of the Wall

Hadrian's Wall is the most important monument built by the Romans in Britain. It is the best-known frontier in the entire Roman Empire and stands today as a reminder of the past glories of one of the world's greatest powers.

Some 1,850 years ago, the Roman Empire covered much of the then known world. It stretched from north Britain eastwards for 2,500 miles to present-day Iraq and southwards to the Sahara desert 1,500 miles away. For 300 years Hadrian's Wall was the north-west frontier of that empire.

Roman armies first invaded Britain under Julius Caesar in 55 BC, but permanent conquest only began in AD 43. In that year the Emperor Claudius launched an invasion of the island. Forty years later, the Romans defeated the Caledonians at the Battle of Mons Graupius and the conquest of the island seemed complete. Subsequent reverses on the Danube led to troop withdrawals from Britain and thus, shortly after AD 100, the northernmost army units in Britain lay along the Tyne–Solway isthmus. Across the isthmus a road, now known as the Stanegate,

provided ready communication between Corbridge and Carlisle, both situated on important north–south routes.

It was on this line in the 120s that the Emperor Hadrian ordered the construction of the Wall that now bears his name. When eventually completed, Hadrian's Wall ran for 80 Roman miles (73 modern miles or 117 km) from Wallsend on the River Tyne to Bowness on the Solway Firth and was of stone throughout its length.

The prior existence of the Stanegate, as well as the geography of the area, governed the

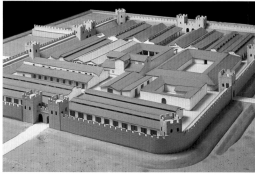

position of the Wall. It ran along the crags in front of the Stanegate from Sewingshields to Carvoran. To the east of Sewingshields it headed for the vantage-point of Limestone Corner and then turned to make for Newcastle. After crossing the North Tyne at Chesters, it followed the northern rim of the Tyne Valley. West of Carvoran the Wall crossed the Irthing at Willowford and lay forward of the river until, at Carlisle, the relationship was reversed and for its last 15 miles the Wall ran along behind the Solway.

As first planned, Hadrian's Wall was to consist of a stone wall (normally bonded in clay) running from the River Tyne to the River Irthing, a

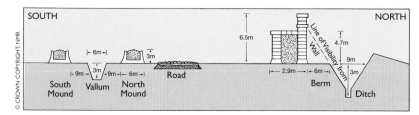

SOUTH   NORTH
6.5m
Line of Visibility from Wall
4.7m
9m
|– 6m –|
|– 9m –| 3m |–9m–|– 6m –| 3m |– 2.9m –|– 6m –| 3m
South   Vallum   North   Road   Berm
Mound   Mound   Ditch

© CROWN COPYRIGHT, NMR

© CROWN COPYRIGHT, NMR

distance of 45 Roman miles. From the Irthing to the Solway, the Wall was built of turf blocks. This was not an impenetrable barrier, for at mile intervals there were gates, each defended by a small guard post, known today as milecastles. Two towers (turrets) were placed between each pair of milecastles, for observation, and it is probable that there was a tower over the north gate of each milecastle, ensuring an unbroken pattern. The turrets were of stone, on stone and turf walls alike. On the stone wall, the milecastles were of stone; on the turf wall, they were of turf and timber. In front of the Wall lay a ditch, except where the crags and the Solway coast made it superfluous. The material from the ditch was tipped out on the north side to form an outer mound.

The Wall crossed three main rivers, the North Tyne, the Irthing and the Eden. Here bridges were provided to aid lateral communication. Another new bridge was probably built at the same time across the Tyne at Newcastle and named *Pons Aelius* (Aelius was Hadrian's family name).

Originally, the troops based in the milecastles and turrets were probably drawn from the army units stationed behind the Wall, for at first there was no intention to place complete units on the Wall line itself. These regiments would remain in their existing bases in northern Britain, and the Wall was built as a separate, and additional, element to the frontier.

The system of milecastles and turrets was continued for at least another 26 miles down the Cumbrian coast to Maryport. No wall was built here and, although in some places the frontier line appears to have been defined by a pair of ditches, the sea was considered a sufficient barrier.

This first plan for Hadrian's Wall was never completed. While work was still in progress a number of modifications were made. First, it was decided to move some regiments up on to the Wall itself. The new forts built at this time lay astride the Wall wherever possible. Secondly, behind the Wall was now constructed the Vallum, a great earthwork stretching along the whole length of the frontier from the Tyne to the Solway. This probably served as the Roman equivalent of barbed wire, defining the rear of the military zone. Crossings through the Vallum were provided, but only at forts; no provision was made for crossing at milecastles. In order to construct both forts and Vallum, troops were taken off building the Wall. When they returned to the Wall, its width was reduced from the original 10 Roman feet to 8 feet or less, presumably to speed up progress. This was not the last alteration to be made to Hadrian's Wall. One or two more forts were added, including Carrawburgh, and a start was made on rebuilding the turf wall in stone, to be completed later in the century. Also later a road, the Military Way, was constructed behind the Wall, linking the forts.

Examples of most of the elements of Hadrian's Wall are in the care of English Heritage and are described in the guidebook.

LEFT: *The Wall at Willowford, looking east. The Wall and ditch are separated by a strip of ground 20 feet wide*

BELOW: *This section across the turf wall shows that it was constructed of turf blocks. The traces of Roman grass survive as dark lines capping the lighter coloured earth of the turfs*

BELOW: *Aerial view of Hadrian's Wall at Cawfields, looking east. Cawfields milecastle lies bottom left and the Wall runs on along the crags. The Vallum follows the easier ground to the right*

WHAT WAS THE WALL FOR?

There were two separate elements to Hadrian's Wall. One was the barrier itself together with the milecastles and turrets. The other was represented by the forts. The function of the barrier, in the words of Hadrian's biographer, was to separate the Romans and the barbarians. The purpose of the regiments stationed in the forts was to protect the province from attack. The distinction between these two roles is emphasized by the first plan for the Wall. In that scheme no regiments were stationed on the barrier itself.

We know little of how the command structure operated on Hadrian's Wall, but we assume that each regiment would supervise its own locality, but in the event of an attack on the province, several could combine to form a force capable of countering an attack in the field, where the Romans were pre-eminent. In such circumstances mobility was important and a barrier of little help.

Hadrian's Wall had a rather different role: frontier control. We know from other frontiers that barbarians – as the Romans called the

RIGHT: The Ermine Street Guard, a modern reconstruction society, display their auxiliary uniforms

Roman forts in northern Britain in AD 130

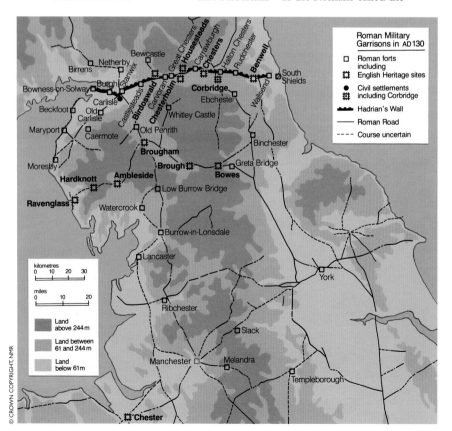

people beyond their boundaries – could only enter the empire unarmed, proceeding under military escort to specified markets, where fees were payable. One function of the Wall was to ensure that these regulations were kept. Another role, no doubt, was to put a stop to the casual disturbances endemic on frontiers, such as small-scale raiding.

Hadrian's Wall did not operate like a medieval town wall: the two were designed to serve different ends. The medieval town wall protected a community of people within a defended circuit. Hadrian's Wall ran for 73 miles across open country serving as a demarcation line. There is no evidence that there was a patrol walk along the top of the Wall; some Roman frontiers were merely fences and so could not be controlled in this way. In any case Roman soldiers, unlike their medieval successors, were not best equipped to fight defensively from the tops of walls. Indeed there were not enough soldiers available to man the Wall in sufficient numbers to defend it adequately from an enemy which might attack in strength at any one point.

Hadrian's Wall and the army of the North were but two elements in the protection of the

© CROWN COPYRIGHT, NMR

ROMAN FORTS

Roman forts tended to be constructed within the same basic framework, though differing in details. The shape corresponds to that of a playing card – a rectangle with rounded corners. The ramparts were of stone or turf, additional defence being provided by ditches, usually two in number. Each side was pierced by a gate, and at regular intervals along the circuit of the rampart was a tower.

The headquarters building lay in the centre of the fort. Its alignment governed the direction the fort faced, usually the enemy, as in the case of most Wall forts, or the rising sun, as at Housesteads. This was the focal point of the fort, and included an assembly hall, administrative rooms and a temple containing a statue of the emperor and the regiment's standards; the strong room was often here too. Normally to the right lay the commanding officer's residence, a large peristyle house in the Mediterranean fashion, and to the left a pair of granaries. A hospital might lie within the central range. The rest of the fort contained barrack blocks, storehouses, a workshop and a latrine; the bath house was outside the enclosure. One building was not provided: a communal mess hall or canteen. It would appear that the soldiers cooked their own food and ate it, perhaps, on the verandah outside their barrack rooms or within the rooms themselves.

Aerial view of Chesters Roman fort in the snow

province. In later years, the existence of Roman army scouts patrolling north of the Wall is recorded and it seems possible that some surveillance was carried out from the time of the Wall's construction. Rome often concluded treaties with the tribes beyond her boundaries. Towards the end of the second century, the long arm of Roman diplomacy stretched over 100 miles (160 km) beyond the Wall to the Caledonians, with whom the Romans concluded a treaty, and this may not have been the first such alliance. These relationships were sometimes strengthened through the payment of subsidies. Rome was well versed in the diplomatic, as well as the martial, arts.

RIGHT: This hoard of nearly 2000 silver denarii was buried at Falkirk near to the abandoned Antonine Wall in or soon after 235. The hoard may have been formed from subsidies paid by the Romans to local chiefs

TRUSTEES OF THE NATIONAL MUSEUMS OF SCOTLAND

WHO BUILT HADRIAN'S WALL?

The construction of Hadrian's Wall was carried out almost entirely by soldiers from the three legions of the province: the Second based at Caerleon near Newport in south Wales, the Sixth from York and the Twentieth stationed at Chester. It is a common fallacy to envisage the Wall being built by slave labour. This was not a practice followed by the Roman army. Within their ranks the legions contained architect-engineers, surveyors, masons, carpenters and glaziers – in short, all the skills required for even the most massive building task. Nevertheless it is not impossible that local civilians were drafted in to aid in transporting materials.

BUILDING TOOLS

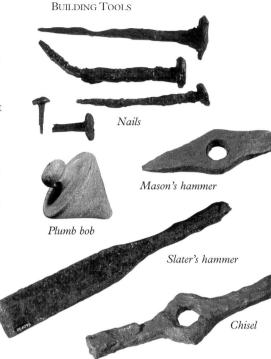

Nails

Mason's hammer

Plumb bob

Slater's hammer

Chisel

BELOW: This inscription from a granary in the fort at Benwell records that it was built for the Emperor Caesar Trajan Hadrian Augustus, under A. Platorius Nepos, governor

MUSEUM OF ANTIQUITIES, NEWCASTLE

RIGHT: This stone, outside Chesters Museum, is from a Roman quarry on Fallowfield Fell about half a mile (1 km) south of Hadrian's Wall. A mason has carved on it 'Petra Flavi Carantini', the rock of Flavius Carantinus. The stone for Hadrian's Wall was obtained locally from quarries such as the one where this inscription was found. Building materials – mortar, water and timber, as well as stone – would have been transported to the Wall in carts or on the backs of mules

RIGHT: This diploma (certificate of privileges), now in the British Museum, was issued on 17 July 122 to Gemellus, son of Breucus, who had just retired from the ala I Pannoniorum Tampiana. He had been discharged by the previous governor Pompeius Falco, but the diploma was not issued until A. Platorius Nepos had assumed office. This dates the arrival of Nepos very closely. The facsimile of a diploma dating to 146 and found at Chesters can be seen in the museum at that site

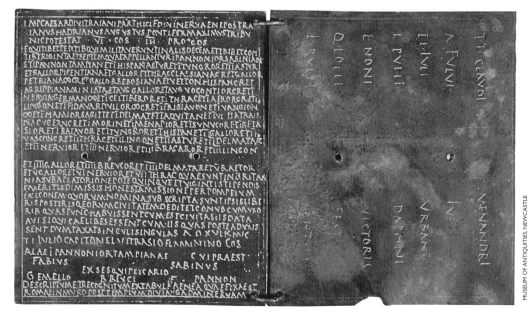

MUSEUM OF ANTIQUITIES, NEWCASTLE

The building of Hadrian's Wall was to occupy the legionaries for at least six years, and modifications were still being carried out at the time of Hadrian's death in 138. As so often happens, the scale of the building project grew and thus yet more soldiers were drafted in to help. These included men from auxiliary units, the other main branch of the provincial army, and also from the British fleet.

The construction of Hadrian's Wall would not have been a costly venture for the imperial treasury. The builders were soldiers already employed by the State while the materials were there for the taking, if not actually imperial property. If built by civilian contractors, the cost of the Wall would have been astronomical, probably well over £100 million at today's prices.

MUSEUM OF ANTIQUITIES, NEWCASTLE

LEFT: An inscription, found at milecastle 38, records that it was built for the Emperor Caesar Trajan Hadrian Augustus by legion II Augusta under A. Platorius Nepos, governor

BELOW: This scene on Trajan's Column in Rome shows legionaries building a fort rampart of turf and digging the surrounding ditch

MANSELL COLLECTION, GETTY IMAGES

WHO WAS HADRIAN?

RIGHT: Bronze head of Emperor Hadrian, found in the Thames

BRITISH MUSEUM

FAR RIGHT: Statue base to the Discipline of the Emperors, erected at Corbridge and dedicated by soldiers of legion II Augusta

It was in 122 that Hadrian came to visit Britain, one of the many stops on a tour of the western provinces of the Roman Empire, and it was probably during this visit that he ordered the construction of the Wall. He wished to consolidate, rather than to extend, the limits of his empire. He was content to see it prosper within the boundaries he had inherited; indeed, he even gave up some of the conquests of his relation and predecessor, Trajan.

Hadrian appreciated two important facts relevant to the safety of his people: the army must be continually trained so that it was ready to defend the empire at any time, and the construction of artificial frontiers would help prevent disruption of life in the frontier areas by unruly elements beyond. Thus Hadrian spent considerable time inspecting the army, supervising its training and improving morale; he also fostered the religious cult of Discipline.

HADRIAN (AD 76–138)

Hadrian was born in Rome in 76, the son of a senator from Italica in Spain. He would have led the normal life of a nobleman in the emperor's service but for the fact that his father's cousin, Trajan, was chosen to succeed the Emperor Nerva in 98. Trajan was childless and Hadrian became the heir presumptive, ascending to the purple in 117.

In Hadrian's view, his predecessor had been too ambitious and some of his conquests were now relinquished. Hadrian, however, went further, establishing artificial frontiers in Germany and Britain, no doubt

WERNER FORMAN ARCHIVE

One of the pools in Hadrian's Villa at Tivoli in Italy. Its design and decoration reflected Hadrian's great interest in Greek art and architecture

© DONALD CORNER & JENNY YOUNG/GREAT BUILDINGS.COM

The Pantheon, Rome, rebuilt by Hadrian

intended to be permanent. He was a great traveller, visiting many parts of his empire. In 121 he was in Germany, and the following year in Britain, where, according to a much later biographer, 'he put many things to rights, and was the first to build a wall, eighty miles long, to separate the Romans from the barbarians'. His visit to the island was commemorated in a poem by Florus: 'I would not like to be Caesar, to walk through Britain.'

Hadrian died at Baia near Naples in 138 and the following year his ashes were placed in the great mausoleum he had erected for himself in Rome. This was turned into a fortress in the Middle Ages, and is now known as Castel Sant'Angelo.

WHO MANNED HADRIAN'S WALL?

The most persistent myth about Hadrian's Wall is that it was guarded by soldiers from Rome or Italy. In fact, the troops based in the forts and milecastles of the Wall were mostly recruited from the north-western provinces of the Roman Empire. The units might have had exotic names, such as *ala I Pannoniorum* which had originally been raised in Pannonia (modern Hungary) or *cohors I Thracum* from Thrace (modern Bulgaria), but once posted to Britain the regiments started recruiting locally. Thus, by the time of Hadrian, many soldiers stationed on the Wall could have been British. Nevertheless, the army of Britain continued to receive some recruits from the Continent and throughout the history of the province there were always a number of Gauls and Germans, for example, serving in the island.

Although mainly built by legionaries, the Wall was manned by auxiliaries. These were the second line troops of the Roman army and their name literally meant 'helpers'. Each fort on the Wall appears to have been built to hold a single auxiliary unit. There were six different sizes and types of auxiliary regiments and all are attested on the Wall. The most common type of unit was the 500-strong mixed infantry and cavalry regiment. This appears to have been the multi-purpose unit of the Roman army. The 500-strong infantry regiment was also well represented.

Cavalry regiments were comparatively rare on Hadrian's Wall and perhaps this reflects the variety of functions that the Wall units had to perform. Nevertheless, the only British example of the most prestigious type of auxiliary unit, the 1000-strong cavalry regiment, was based on the Wall, at Stanwix near Carlisle. Its commanding officer was the highest ranking officer on the Wall line, but that does not imply that he had any special authority over the other commanding officers on the frontier. There is no evidence for any local command hierarchy and it is not known what part the legionary legate at York played in the command structure. It seems highly probable, nevertheless, that some system existed for co-ordination and combination of units.

The commanding officers of auxiliary units were drawn from the gentry and aristocracy of the empire. They came to their first appointments with little, if any, military experience, and many did not receive further appointments. These men moved freely about the empire commanding regiments and a few rose to the very pinnacle of the imperial civil service.

Infantry units were divided into *centuriae* (centuries), each probably 80 strong (the old link to 100 had long been lost), while the cavalry was subdivided into troops, each probably containing 32 men. The infantry was led by centurions, the cavalry by decurions. These officers had generally risen from the ranks and they formed a professional officer core to the army. They also provided continuity since the commanding officers were career postings, each usually held for about three years. Each centurion and decurion would normally have had at least 15 years service in the ranks. A few, however, were appointed to their posts directly from civilian life. Centurions and decurions might have continued in post for decades; the longest known tenure of office by a legionary centurion is 61 years.

ABOVE: Auxiliary infantryman (right) and cavalryman from the first century AD; drawn by Peter Connolly

CENTRE: Many units had a symbol. The boar was the emblem of the Twentieth Legion

BELOW: The tombstone of an archer in an unknown regiment from Housesteads

9

MILITARY LIFE ON THE WALL

TOP: Samian cup, made in Gaul (France)
ABOVE: Bowl and jars made in Britain and found at Corbridge

ABOVE RIGHT: The remains of two ovens, built on the ground floor of the east tower of the south gate at Birdoswald

RIGHT: Recruits training outside a fort, drawn by Peter Connolly

There is no contemporary evidence to illustrate daily life on Hadrian's Wall. We do not know how long particular duties lasted or what sort of distances were covered by soldiers on patrol. Nevertheless, on the basis of evidence from other parts of the Roman Empire, we can say something about life on the Wall.

The soldier's day started with breakfast. This may have been something like our porridge. The main meal of the day was in the evening. The Roman soldier had a varied diet, eating bread, soup, meat, fish, fruit and vegetables, and drinking beer and cheap wine.

Part of the day might have been given over to training. Roman military manuals stressed that all soldiers should receive regular weapons drill, physical training and should participate in military exercises. Special cavalry exercises included mock battles; those performed by the Roman army in Africa in 128 were observed by the Emperor Hadrian.

Many soldiers would be occupied for at least part of the day with fatigues. These included guard duty, cleaning the centurion's uniform and looking after the bath house. All such tasks were recorded both on duty rosters and on soldiers' files. In the Roman army, even horses had their own records, while receipts had to be completed in quadruplicate! Some soldiers had special jobs in the building as maintenance staff or in the regimental office; others were adjutants, standard bearers, or buglers who sounded the watch and indicated orders on the march.

There would always have been some soldiers on duty – or ill – at the fort but many would have been serving elsewhere. Supplies in transit needed protecting while some regiments sent men to serve on the governor's staff in London. The main activity, however, was probably patrolling, either along the Wall or in the lands to the north. Surveillance would have been maintained over the tribes beyond the frontier, many probably being in treaty relationship with Rome. We know from other frontiers that treaties might strictly define the time and place of a tribe's assembly and that it should be supervised by a Roman officer. Such activities might have taken soldiers far beyond the Wall.

© CROWN COPYRIGHT, NMR

GRANARIES

The Roman historian Tacitus, writing a few years before the construction of Hadrian's Wall, remarked that forts should contain sufficient supplies to last for a year. The primary storehouses for food were the granaries. The floors of these were raised to help keep the food fresh and dry and restrict access by rodents. Vents in the exterior walls allowed the circulation of air. The other key feature of the granaries are the buttresses supporting the walls. These were probably erected in order to provide stability for the long walls, otherwise unsupported by partitions. It is not clear whether grain was stored in bins or sacks, which certainly existed in the Roman world.

While cereals formed the staple part of the diet, soldiers also ate meat (cattle, sheep, pig and other animals), fish, shellfish, vegetables (lentils, cabbage, peas, beans, carrots and celery), nuts and fruit (apples, pears, plums, cherries, peaches, grapes, apricots, strawberries and raspberries). Seasoning, such as coriander and opium poppy, might have been brought from afar – from the Continent in some cases. Wine and beer were both drunk, though where they were stored is not known.

ABOVE: Model of a granary

RIGHT: Bronze corn measure, found at Carvoran, which may have measured a soldier's weekly ration of corn, and could be early official use of the seven-day week

LEFT: A corn mill, found at Chesters

THE BATH HOUSE

The Romans understood that a group of men housed together were susceptible to disease, hence hygiene was an important concern. Each fort appears to have been provided with a flushing latrine, and many with a hospital. The other important building was the bath house. This was normally located outside the fort, presumably because of the fire risk.

Many bath houses offered two forms of bathing: the steam treatment or Turkish bath (so-called because the Turks took it over when they conquered Constantinople), and the hot dry bath or sauna. Soldiers first entered the changing room, and then had the choice of bathing. Each room was hotter than the last, the final room being situated over the furnace. The fires here heated the basement below the floors, hence sandals had to be worn. The hot air passed through vents up the walls to escape at the roof. Stone benches allowed the soldiers to relax,

and perhaps play board games. Their bodies would be anointed with oil and the dirt and oil scraped off with a blunt knife or strigil. After such treatment, the soldier could take a dip in the cold bath before returning to the fort.

LEFT: This glass flask, found at Corbridge, carried the oil used in bath houses. Oil was used instead of soap

BELOW: A reconstruction of the regimental bath house at Chesters, by Alan Sorrell

THE SOLDIER'S PERSONAL LIFE

RIGHT: A gaming board, dice, dice-shakers and counters, all found at Corbridge

BOTTOM RIGHT: The Rudge Cup dates from the second century. Above what may be a depiction of Hadrian's Wall is a list of the forts in the western half of the Wall. This was presumably one of two or three vessels naming all the forts along the frontier. They were enamelled and probably made to be sold as souvenirs

BELOW: In the third century, a flourishing civil settlement grew up outside the fort at Housesteads. This reconstruction by Alan and Richard Sorrell shows the main street towards the south gate of the fort with half-timbered houses on either side

Every army has its followers. They followed Caesar around Gaul, and others no doubt arrived in Britain in the wake of Claudius's army in AD 43. As the army moved north, it was presumably accompanied by various civilians who set up house outside the new forts.

One important group in the civil settlement would have been the soldiers' families. During the second century, a Roman soldier was not allowed to marry, but there was nothing to stop him from contracting a union with a woman according to local law, and such 'marriages' were subsequently recognized in Roman law when the soldier retired, and his children were legitimized. Inscriptions record soldiers' wives, children, fathers, mothers, sisters and brothers.

The Roman soldier was relatively well paid, and he attracted people who wanted to part him from his money. These included merchants selling food and wine, clothing, pottery and knick-knacks.

There was no such thing as the weekend or 48-hour pass in the Roman army. Soldiers had to apply to their centurions for leave and frequently bribed them to obtain it. We do not know how often leave might have been obtained. Similarly, we know nothing about the number of hours a soldier might have been expected to work each day. We do know that there were a number of religious festivals throughout the year – perhaps 50 in total – and these may have been treated as holidays.

It may be suspected that in general soldiers would try to get away with doing as little work as possible – and obtain as much as possible from civilians without payment. This natural state of affairs was exacerbated by the perennial problem of the peace-time army; as it was not fighting, it had little to do. When Corbulo took over the army of Syria, he found (according to Tacitus), that it contained soldiers who had never been on guard duty and did not possess armour. Good emperors and generals, such as Hadrian, tried to compensate for this inactivity by training and manoeuvres. Nevertheless, it would not be surprising if the civilian settlement was as much a home to the soldier as the fort itself.

© CROWN COPYRIGHT, NMR

RELIGION IN THE ROMAN ARMY

Religious belief is represented on the Wall at both official and personal level. Dedications were often made to Jupiter (as well as to Juno and Minerva). At Maryport there is a unique collection of dedications to Jupiter by the commanding officers of the First Cohort of Spaniards. Special ceremonies were held at the beginning of each year, on the emperor's birthday and on the anniversary of the emperor's succession – 10 July in the case of Hadrian. On that day, prayers were made to the gods for the wellbeing of the emperor and the oath of allegiance was administered to the troops.

Personal religion was often in the form of a bargain with the gods. A soldier going on a journey, for example, vowed that if a particular god preserved his life, he would dedicate an altar to that god or sacrifice an animal, or even build a shrine. Some of these gods were local, and unique to this area, such as Antenociticus, Belatucadrus, Cocidius and the Veteres. Sometimes these gods were equated with Roman gods, thus Mars with Belatucadrus and Apollo with Maponus. Other gods were introduced to the area by incoming units, such as Mars Thincsus at Housesteads. The temples of these gods were small buildings, for religion was a personal affair, not the occasion for a public gathering.

Eastern mystery religions are also represented on Hadrian's Wall. The most famous is Mithraism. Temples to Mithras have been excavated at Rudchester, Housesteads and Carrawburgh, where it is still visible. These temples may have been singled out for special destruction by Christians, who saw Mithraism as a parody of their own beliefs.

ABOVE: The head of a Celtic horned god found at the outpost fort at Netherby

TOP LEFT: A head of the god Hercules found at Housesteads; this would once have adorned a temple

LEFT: A silver plaque dedicated to the god Cocidius, a local version of Mars. It was found in the strong room of the headquarters building at Bewcastle

LEFT: This altar found at Housesteads, together with an arch, neatly demonstrates the all-embracing nature of Roman religion, being dedicated to the Roman god Mars, the German goddesses Alaisiagae and the deity of the Emperor by German soldiers in the Frisian unit based at the fort

FAR LEFT: Each of these gods wears the cucullus, a local cloak rather like a duffel coat but without sleeves. The sculpture can be seen in the museum at Housesteads

HOW DID THE WALL AFFECT THE LOCAL PEOPLE?

RIGHT: The Knag Burn gate at Housesteads. Access was through a narrow passage, which had doors at both ends and was flanked by a guard chamber on either side

Contemporary written sources for Hadrian's Wall are scarce, and they tell us nothing about the local people whose lives would have been drastically affected by this massive building project. Archaeology, however, seems to provide positive evidence for at least one result of the construction of the Wall. At Milking Gap, one mile west of Housesteads, between the Wall and the Vallum, a farmhouse was abandoned, probably because it now lay within the military zone: here the hand of the army may be suspected.

ABOVE: The Romano-British settlement at Milking Gap from the air. The ruins of five round stone houses lie within and beside the farmyard wall, also built of stone

The Wall would have had an effect on farming rather similar to a modern motorway that slices through farmland, destroying old access routes and cutting off fields from the farmsteads. Possibly the Knag Burn gate at Housesteads was broken through the Wall to provide ease of movement for farmers and their beasts.

The building of Hadrian's Wall increased the number of troops based in this part of Britain. The soldiers required feeding and the army preferred to obtain its supplies locally. Thus it might be expected that the arrival of the Roman army in northern Britain in the late first century, and then its strengthening under Hadrian, would lead to changes in local farming patterns and particularly increased cereal production. There is some archaeological evidence to support this assumption, but unfortunately there has not yet been enough work in this field of research to quantify any change.

One major change brought about by the presence of so many Roman soldiers on the Wall was the growth of the settlements outside forts. As well as the soldiers' families and merchants, these may also have attracted farmers from the northern countryside; the army probably attracted local boys too as recruits. No evidence for either survives, though a Brigantian is known to have served on the Antonine Wall. Certainly, Roman objects found in Roman forts demonstrate some contact between soldier and civilian but the nature of this is unclear.

Rome would have imposed peace (and taxation) on the north, putting an end to the ritualized warfare so beloved of the Celts. This peace would have extended well beyond the Wall into the areas under Roman surveillance. The presence of the army was not wholly advantageous to the local people. Numerous contemporary documents from other parts of the empire record the extortion and theiving ways of Roman soldiers. Other documents show that while the army might have brought peace it could not wholly eradicate pillaging. Dealing with such activities fell to the army in the absence of a police force in the Roman Empire and would have been another duty drawing soldiers away from the Wall.

RIGHT: Model of the Romano-British farm at Riding Wood, Northumberland. Three round houses sit within a walled enclosure; the yards would have served as pens for cattle or sheep. The surrounding wall would have helped to keep out wild animals such as wolves and bears

THE LATER ROMAN HISTORY OF THE WALL

Remarkably, within months of Hadrian's death in July 138, his successor, Antoninus Pius, had decided to abandon the newly built Wall and move the frontier forward by nearly 100 miles (160 km), building a new wall across the Forth–Clyde isthmus. This new wall, the Antonine Wall, was built of turf throughout its length of 40 Roman miles (37 modern miles = 60 km). Following another change of emperor, however, it too was abandoned after about 20 years, this time in favour of a return to Hadrian's Wall.

In the 160s, Hadrian's Wall was reoccupied. The Wall and its buildings were repaired and the ditches cleaned out. One new feature was added – a road, the Military Way. Previously the Stanegate, running a mile or so behind the Wall along the river valleys, had been the main line of communication across the isthmus.

Twenty years later, there began a troublesome time for the Wall. There was a major invasion of the province by the northern tribes; victory took four years to achieve. In 197, the new governor found both the principal barbarian tribes in the north, the Caledones and the Maeatae, eager for war. Unable to mount an offensive himself, he had to purchase peace by the payment of a considerable sum of money. Even so, trouble rumbled on in the north for the next ten years.

In 208, the Emperor Septimius Severus came to Britain with his two sons, intent on solving the problem of the British frontier for good. His aim was to complete the conquest of the island. He campaigned against the Caledones and Maeatae and forced them to submit, but at the time of his death at York in February 211 both tribes were in revolt. His sons reversed his policy, making treaties with the enemy, evacuating their territory, and returning to Rome.

Throughout the third century, little is heard of north Britain. So far as we can tell, the frontier was at peace. But, at the very end of the century, in 297, we first hear of the new enemy that was to menace the northern frontier – the Picts. There were several campaigns against them during the fourth century, some led by the emperor himself. Trouble in the 360s peaked in a conspiracy of all

the barbarian tribes in 367. Order was restored and the defences repaired, by Count Theodosius.

Hadrian's Wall slid into obscurity; it did not end in catastrophe. In 407 the British army chose its own emperor, Constantine III, and he also departed for the Continent to try to win the imperial throne. He probably took his field army and other troops with him. Britain became cut off from the rest of the empire and rule from Rome was never restored.

No mass evacuation of Roman troops and officials took place. British cities – the basis of local government in the island – were left to manage their own affairs. It is doubtful if the army on the Wall was withdrawn in 407. It was no longer a mobile force, merely a static frontier garrison. When the pay chests failed to arrive, the soldiers would have turned to other activities such as farming and pillaging, while others may have left to seek opportunities elsewhere. The Wall was left to decay.

ABOVE: The Picts have left many records on their enigmatic symbol stones. This stone, from Aberlemno, and probably dating to the eighth century, shows a group of Picts hunting. The Pictish nation was formed by the amalgamation of the tribes earlier recorded occupying the land north of the Forth, including the Caledones

ABOVE LEFT: The Antonine Wall was built in the 140s from Bo'ness on the Forth to Old Kilpatrick on the Clyde. Its main surviving feature today is the ditch. This view shows the ditch crossing Croy Hill

CENTRE: Coin showing the Emperor Constantius, who campaigned against the Picts shortly before his death in 306

BELOW: Turret 41a was eliminated in the late second century when the Wall was rebuilt across its site. The original internal north wall of the turret can be seen behind the later wall blocking the recess

AFTER THE ROMANS LEFT

Nearly a thousand inscriptions on stone have been found on Hadrian's Wall. These have been carefully recorded and published. This inscription was found at Birdoswald fort in 1821 and first published in the Carlisle Patriot on 16 June 1821. The altar was dedicated to the holy god Silvanus by the venatores Bannienses, which was probably a regiment based at Birdoswald in the third century. Silvanus was god of the woods

We know very little of life on Hadrian's Wall during the centuries following its abandonment by Rome. The English (Anglo-Saxons) began to take over in southern and eastern England in the fifth and sixth centuries, and, in the north, in the late sixth and seventh centuries. North of the Wall, it was in the fifth century that the Scots from Ireland began to settle on the west coast of the country that was later named after them, Scotland.

A few Anglo-Saxon objects have been found towards the east end of Hadrian's Wall, but in the main the newcomers largely passed it by. More evidence about the later history of the forts is coming to light. The tombstone of Brigomaglos, dating to about 500, has long been known at *Vindolanda*. Excavations at Birdoswald have indicated that some buildings continued in occupation beyond 400, when the fort may have become the base of a chieftain.

DEOSANCTO SILVANO VE NATORES BANNESS

The Wall is also recorded in the literature of the time. Gildas, writing about 540, knew of both Hadrian's Wall and the Antonine Wall, but placed their construction 250 years too late and thought they had been built against the Picts and Scots, an erroneous view of the function of Hadrian's Wall that has persisted to the present day. The Venerable Bede, in his *History of the English Church and People*, completed in 731, followed Gildas on the date and function of Hadrian's Wall, but added the information that it was eight feet wide and twelve high. These dimensions may well have resulted from his own observations as his monastery lay close to the eastern end of the Wall.

Through the centuries that followed, the Wall was frequently plundered for stone used to build the churches, houses and field walls of northern England. Stones were carried many miles: inscriptions from Birdoswald have been found

DAVID J BREEZE

The 1886 pilgrims at Lanercost Priory. This was the second Pilgrimage – the first was in 1849. John Collingwood Bruce, now an old man, is seated on the right, wearing his usual shepherd's plaid

MUSEUM OF ANTIQUITIES, NEWCASTLE

5 miles (8 km) away at Lanercost Priory, for example. This use of the Wall as a convenient quarry continued into the late nineteenth century. Despoilers occasionally sought other plunder. During the reign of King John, in 1201, there was an excavation to seek treasure but none was found. In later centuries, the local gentry carried off inscriptions and sculpture to adorn their houses.

The era of serious observation and enquiry began in the sixteenth century and early antiquarian accounts are still useful sources of information about the Wall. It was only in 1840, however, that the whole of the frontier complex was first correctly attributed to Hadrian, though this was not immediately generally accepted. It was also about this time that archaeological excavations began on the Wall.

EARLY ARCHAEOLOGISTS AND HISTORIANS OF THE WALL

Visitors to Hadrian's Wall have been recording their impressions since the sixteenth century. One of the more remarkable was William Hutton who, at the age of 78 in 1801, walked from Birmingham to Carlisle, and from there to Bowness, to Wallsend, back to Carlisle and then home – a journey of 601 miles, as he proudly recorded.

The modern study of Hadrian's Wall can be said to have started in the middle of the nineteenth century. In 1840, John Hodgson, curate of Jarrow, finally determined that the Wall was actually built on the orders of Hadrian. In 1849, John Collingwood Bruce, a schoolmaster and minister in Newcastle, led the first tour or pilgrimage along the Wall and two years later published his first edition of *The Roman Wall*. Finally, between 1852 and 1854 Henry MacLaughlan surveyed the whole frontier, producing a map that was not superseded until the publication of the first ordnance survey map of Hadrian's Wall in 1964.

Another of the great leaders of Wall studies at this time was John Clayton of Chesters. He inherited the Chesters estate in 1832 and steadily expanded his holding along the Wall so that by his death in 1890 he owned five forts. He had his workman uncover and rebuild many miles of the frontier and excavate several buildings, including Coventina's Well and the bath house at Carrawburgh, Black Carts turret (29a), the milecastles at Housesteads (37) and Cawfields (42), Chesters bridge and parts of Chesters fort. The museum at Chesters, though not built until after his death, is essentially his collection of relics.

Modern excavation can be said to have started in the 1890s with the investigation of Mucklebank Turret (44b), the examination of Housesteads fort and a campaign of work led by Professor Haverfield, aimed at elucidating the history and relationship of the various linear elements to each other. Some problems took many years to solve, and it was not until the 1930s that the nature of the turf wall was understood. Excavation continues to this day, examining and laying bare the structures that form Hadrian's Wall.

RIGHT: Revd John Hodgson (1779–1845) was the first to suggest that Hadrian's Wall, its forts and the Vallum were all built under Hadrian

MUSEUM OF ANTIQUITIES, NEWCASTLE

ABOVE: John Clayton of Chesters (1792–1890), who did so much to preserve the Wall and reveal its secrets in the nineteenth century

THE 21st-CENTURY CHALLENGE

Excavation in 1999 on the earthworks of the Vallum at Appletree produced significant new information about the history of this earthwork

Many miles of Hadrian's Wall are in the care of English Heritage. Looking after those sections is a full-time task. Here a mason is consolidating a length of Wall

Modern excavation began in the 1890s and still continues. During the years up to 1939, many of the major problems concerning the Wall were solved through excavation. Nevertheless, there still remain large areas where our knowledge is very imperfect, in particular concerning the history and layout of forts and the history of the whole Wall through the third and fourth centuries, while, with the exception of *Vindolanda*, civil settlements have been little explored, and cemeteries not at all.

It was in 1933 that Corbridge was taken into the care of the nation and this was followed in 1934 by part of Hadrian's Wall. Since that date, several miles of the Wall, including turrets, milecastles and forts, have come into State care; they are all now looked after by English Heritage. In addition, other parts of the Wall are owned by local authorities, including the forts at South Shields, Wallsend, Rudchester and Birdoswald, while the National Trust owns the fort at Housesteads and the Wall thereabouts. All these fragments of the great frontier complex built over 1,850 years ago are carefully preserved in the public interest and open to visitors.

A monument like Hadrian's Wall requires continual attention. Mortar decays and requires replacing. The pressure of feet on turf leads to erosion of grass and then soil. Visitors climbing on walls dislodge stones. Interpretation moves on and information panels need renewing. New discoveries lead to the necessity to upgrade site displays and museums. Thus, the staff of English Heritage, the National Trust, Tyne and Wear Museums Service, the Vindolanda Trust and other bodies concerned with Hadrian's Wall are kept busy.

For archaeologists, Hadrian's Wall is an incomparable archaeological resource. Over one hundred years of scientific excavation, and before that observation and recording, has led to the creation of a vast body of material capable of being re-examined and reassessed. In addition, new excavations take place on Hadrian's Wall every year. Each year, our view of this great frontier changes subtly as a result of this work.

The traditional methods of excavation and aerial photography have been supplemented over recent years by remote sensing – geophysical survey in particular – through which a plan of the remains below the ground surface can be produced but without resort to the spade. However, the plan thus produced is undated, and while it may be possible to identify a particular building as Roman, it is not possible to date it within the 300 years of occupation of Hadrian's Wall. Excavation is expensive, though, and geophysical survey offers an exciting way of learning much more about both military and civil structures along the frontier.

The challenge faced by all those concerned with Hadrian's Wall is safeguarding this precious monument so that it continues to be investigated and interpreted, conserved and maintained to the highest standards to the benefit of the monument itself and the enjoyment of visitors.

THE NEW NATIONAL TRAIL

In 1987 Hadrian's Wall was declared a World Heritage Site. In accordance with the requirements of such a designation, English Heritage has prepared and is executing a management plan, in co-operation with many other bodies concerned with Hadrian's Wall.

The provision of access to the Wall took an important step forward in May 2003 with the opening of the national trail along the Wall. Now, for the first time, a footpath exists along the whole line of the Wall and walkers no longer have to brave cars and lorries thundering along the Military Road.

Every ten years, a special tour of the Wall takes place – the Pilgrimage of Hadrian's Wall – organized by the two local archaeological societies, the Society of Antiquaries of Newcastle and the Cumberland and Westmorland Antiquarian and Archaeological Society. In 1999 over 200 Pilgrims celebrated the 150th anniversary of the first Pilgrimage by traversing the frontier from the mouth of the Tyne to Maryport on the Cumbrian Coast.

Sewingshields Carrawburgh
Willowford Cawfields Housesteads
Birdoswald Chesters Heddon-on- South Shields
Walltown Vindolanda Brunton the-Wall NEWCASTLE Roman Fort
owness-on-Solway Turret UPON TYNE
CARLISLE Corbridge Wallsend
Roman Town

EXPLORING
THE WALL

SOUTH SHIELDS *(Arbeia)* ROMAN FORT

The very end of the frontier complex lay at South Shields where a fort sat on the low hill overlooking the mouth of the River Tyne. The archaeological ruins here were first laid out in 1882 as the People's Roman Remains Park; they are now owned by South Tyneside Metropolitan Borough Council and managed on their behalf by Tyne and Wear Museums.

The visible fort at South Shields was probably built under Marcus Aurelius (161–80), replacing an earlier fort dating to the reign of Hadrian. Most of the visible buildings are of local sandstone but in the earliest stages of building, magnesian limestone was used, for example in the double granary. The water settling tanks show that the fort was supplied by an aqueduct. The original west gate was reconstructed to full size between 1986 and 1987.

In the early third century, the south wall of the fort was taken down and the fort extended, increasing its area from 3.9 to 5.1 acres (1.6– 2.1 hectares). Many of the buildings were replaced by 15 granaries. These changes, converting the fort into a supply base, were probably connected with Septimius Severus' campaigns and projected occupation of Scotland. After 211, when the Scottish campaigns ended, its purpose had to change; presumably its use now was to store supplies for the units of the northern frontier and more granaries were built. Several of the granaries and the headquarters building of the supply base are visible.

CENTRE: This inscription records the installation of a water supply for cohors V Gallorum *in 222 during the reign of the Emperor Severus Alexander*

ARBEIA ROMAN FORT, TYNE & WEAR MUSEUMS

ARBEIA ROMAN FORT, TYNE & WEAR MUSEUMS

ABOVE: Tombstone of Victor the Moor, freedman of Numerianus, a cavalryman in the first cavalry regiment of Asturians. Many Roman soldiers appear to have kept slaves

LEFT: A replica of the west gate, rebuilt in 1986 on the original foundations. Detailed research has resulted in the most authentic reconstruction of a fort gate anywhere in the Roman Empire

BELOW: One of a pair of harness mounts found at South Shields

MUSEUM OF ANTIQUITIES, NEWCASTLE

TOUR OF SOUTH SHIELDS *(Arbeia)*

The **entrance** lies through the reconstructed **west gate**, which houses a series of displays. The layout of the fort can best be understood by viewing it from the top of the gate, after which the visitor should proceed to the **north gate** by way of the **north-west angle tower**.

The **headquarters building** dates from the late third or early fourth century. The rear rooms of this building include a strong room (with part of a window sill surviving); the offices on either side contain hypocausts. Behind is the well that lay in the courtyard of the second-century headquarters.

Parts of nine **granaries** are visible in the central area: two preserve the partitions of later barracks. South of the granaries the **headquarters building** associated with the supply base can be seen. Beyond lie the reconstructed **barrack block** and **courtyard house**. Behind may be inspected the junction of the original east **fort wall** and its extension, marked by the remains of the south-east angle tower. Continue past the third-century **communal latrine** to the later **south-east angle**, where the chamfered base

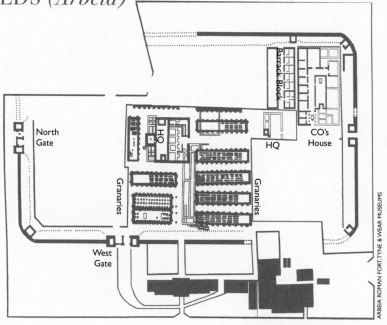

North Gate

HQ

Granaries

Granaries

Barrack Block

CO's House

HQ

West Gate

ARBEIA ROMAN FORT, TYNE & WEAR MUSEUMS

of the fort wall is preserved. Walk on past the **south gate** and **south-west angle tower** to the site **museum and archaeology centre** where recent finds from excavations are displayed and explained.

LEFT: *South Shields fort from the air*

RIGHT: *The communal latrine was provided for the use of all the soldiers in the regiment. The soldiers cleaned themselves with moss or sponges*

BELOW: *One of the granaries built in the early third century to help supply the army campaigning in Scotland. A flagged floor, supported on low walls, was raised to keep the food fresh and dry*

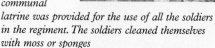

After the buildings of the supply base had been destroyed by fire in the late third or early fourth century, the interior of the fort was completely replanned. Twelve barracks were built in the southern part of the fort, ten of them reusing the walls of the granaries. A new headquarters building was erected on the site of the original headquarters and a large courtyard house, with a dining room and hypocausts, occupied the south-east corner of the fort. This building may be associated with the replacement of *cohors V Gallorum* by a new unit, the *numerus barcariorum Tigrisiensium*, a unit of bargemen from the River Tigris. The house and an adjacent barrack block were rebuilt between 2001 and 2002. Activity in the fort continued into the fifth century and perhaps beyond.

ARBEIA ROMAN FORT, TYNE & WEAR MUSEUMS

LEFT: The plain tombstone of Barathes of Palmyra found at Corbridge and the highly decorated tombstone of Regina, wife of Barathes of Palmyra, from South Shields (far left); the two inscriptions probably refer to the same man. While in Britain, he bought a slave girl, Regina, of the tribe of the Catuvellauni; he freed her and married her. Regina's elaborate tombstone is carved in Palmyrene style

ARBEIA ROMAN FORT, TYNE & WEAR MUSEUMS

FAR LEFT: Most forts contained a strong room, where the unit's and the soldiers' money was kept. The lower stones were held together by cramps

LEFT: Reconstruction of the interior of the commanding officer's house

BELOW LEFT: Reconstruction of a barrack block

BELOW: Mars, the god of war, on a sword found at South Shields

ARBEIA ROMAN FORT, TYNE & WEAR MUSEUMS

ARBEIA ROMAN FORT, TYNE & WEAR MUSEUMS

Bowness-on-Solway
CARLISLE
Birdoswald
Willowford
Cawfields
Walltown
Sewingshields
Housesteads
Carrawburgh
Chesters
Vindolanda
Brunton
Turret
Corbridge
Roman Town
Heddon-on-the-Wall
NEWCASTLE UPON TYNE
South Shields
Roman Fort
Wallsend

WALLSEND (*Segedunum*) ROMAN FORT

TYNE & WEAR MUSEUMS

ABOVE: Cavalry harness fitting with punched inscription

CENTRE: Bronze figurine of the goddess Fortuna

TYNE & WEAR MUSEUMS

ABOVE: Lead portable shrine, probably to the god Mercury and dating from the fourth century

Wallsend, as its name implies, lies at the very end of the Wall. In the nineteenth century, the fort was lost to housing, but, following excavations in 1970, the whole fort has been laid out, reconstructions erected and a new museum and visitor centre opened, making this one of the most exciting sites to visit along the whole Wall. The fort is owned by North Tyneside Metropolitan Borough Council and managed on their behalf by Tyne and Wear Museums Service.

The fort at Wallsend was built under Hadrian. It was the terminal fort, and a short length of Wall ran down from the south-east corner to the river. The internal buildings followed the normal plan, with the headquarters in the centre, flanked to the right by the large courtyard house for the commanding officer and to the left by a double granary. In the later second century, a forehall was built across the front of the headquarters building and the granary, overlying the main road across the fort. The central range also contained a building, thought to be a hospital, to the north of which lay a large water tank.

The rest of the fort mainly contained barrack blocks. Of particular interest is a pair to the south of the central range. These formed a dual function as the accommodation of cavalrymen and their horses. The front rooms of the buildings were the stables, identified by the drains, while the soldiers lived in the rear rooms, which often contained a hearth. The decurion commanding the cavalry troop occupied the suite of rooms at the rampart end of each building.

In the third and fourth centuries, the layout of the fort was altered. The barracks in the southern

TYNE & WEAR MUSEUMS

BELOW: Segedunum from the air. The fort plan is shown as it would have been at the end of the second century. The fort housed a mixed contingent of infantry and cavalry; the barrack blocks for the cavalry are visible at the bottom

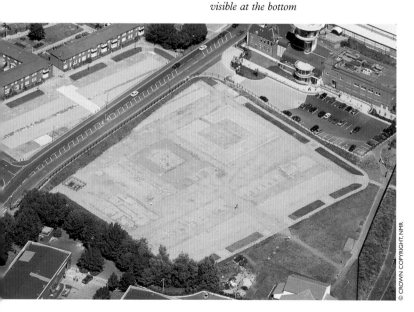

© CROWN COPYRIGHT, NMR

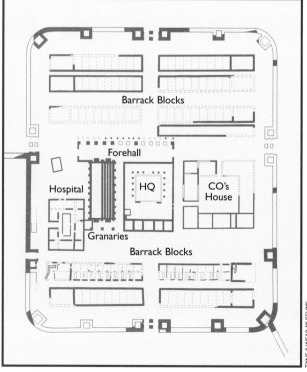

Barrack Blocks

Forehall

Hospital

HQ

CO's House

Granaries

Barrack Blocks

TYNE & WEAR MUSEUMS

LEFT: *Exterior of the
reconstructed bath house*

FAR LEFT: *The* labrum, *or
small fountain, in the hot
room (*caldarium*) of the
reconstructed bath house*

LEFT: *Interior of the bath
house showing the bath
fresco*

BELOW: *Part of a Roman
double toilet seat*

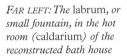

BELOW: *To the west of the
fort, a full-sized replica of
Hadrian's Wall has been
built immediately behind
the original foundations*

part of the fort were replaced by four buildings
of less regular plans, but in a style similar to
contemporary structures elsewhere.

The location of the fort's bath house is not
known, but a replica of such a building, modelled
on that at Chesters, has been erected to the west
of the fort. It gives an excellent impression of
the internal space, otherwise impossible to
achieve, even at Chesters.

Another reconstruction is a section of
Hadrian's Wall. The length of genuine Wall
immediately to the east had collapsed in antiquity
and still exhibits a strange configuration.

The museum offers a display of finds, models
and a viewing platform.

Bowness-on-Solway
CARLISLE
Birdoswald
Willowford Cawfields
Walltown Vindolanda
Sewingshields Carrawburgh
Housesteads
Chesters Brunton
Turret
Corbridge
Roman Town
Heddon-on-the-Wall
NEWCASTLE UPON TYNE
South Shields Roman Fort
Wallsend

NEWCASTLE TO HEDDON-ON-THE-WALL

MUSEUM OF ANTIQUITIES, NEWCASTLE

The head of Antenociticus formerly graced a statue that probably stood in the apse of the temple at Benwell

RIGHT: Denton Hall turret (7b) looking west. The turret is recessed into the thickness of the Wall. To the left is a platform, which may have formed the base for a ladder leading to the first floor and above

A model of the Roman fort at Benwell as it might have appeared. This, and the model of the Vallum crossing, is displayed in the Museum of Antiquities in the University of Newcastle

The Military Road, constructed in the aftermath of the 1745 Jacobite uprising led by Bonnie Prince Charlie, carries the modern visitor westwards from Newcastle. Beside the road are scattered fragments of the Wall. These were all built to the original specification for the Wall, 10 Roman feet thick, often referred to as 'broad wall'.

The fort at Benwell is buried beneath 1930s housing, but two important fragments can be seen. South of the fort, the causeway leading across the Vallum ditch is preserved, while a short distance away, but in a different housing estate, is the temple of a local god, Antenociticus.

A mile to the west, immediately beside the modern road, is Denton Hall turret (7b). Built

of unusually large stones, it still retains the platform in the corner, which probably served as the base for a ladder leading to the upper floors.

At Heddon-on-the-Wall can be seen the longest visible stretch of broad wall, 10 Roman feet thick. The stones here were originally set in clay, but this has now been replaced by mortar for stability. A circular structure in the thickness of the wall is a kiln of post-Roman date.

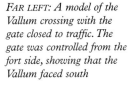

FAR LEFT: A model of the Vallum crossing with the gate closed to traffic. The gate was controlled from the fort side, showing that the Vallum faced south

LEFT: The Vallum crossing at Benwell, looking north-east. The road leading south from the fort passes through the gate. Heavy wear led to repeated resurfacing of the road and this is represented by the steps in its surface. The masonry of the surviving gate pier is amongst the best anywhere on the Wall. The ditch is now only half its original depth

The broad wall and ditch at Heddon-on-the-Wall, looking east. The rubble core of the Wall was usually clay-bonded with only the facing stones mortared. Traces of mortar still adhering to the faces of some stones suggest that the Wall may have looked more white than brown when built

The temple of Antenociticus at Benwell. The altars are copies; the originals are in the Museum of Antiquities, Newcastle

Bowness-on-Solway
CARLISLE
Birdoswald
Willowford Cawfields
Walltown Vindolanda
Sewingshields Carrawburgh
Housesteads
Chesters
Brunton
Turret
Corbridge
Roman Town
Heddon-on-
the-Wall
NEWCASTLE
UPON TYNE
South Shields
Roman Fort
Wallsend

CORBRIDGE ROMAN TOWN *(Coria)*

ABOVE: The Corbridge lion. This once adorned a fountain in a house south of the military compounds. It was probably originally designed for a tomb

CENTRE: The god Taranis. A plaque made from a pottery mould found at Corbridge

BELOW: A reconstruction of Corbridge as it might have been in the early third century, looking west along the Stanegate

This site was occupied longer than any other along the line of Hadrian's Wall. A fort was established here in the 80s and continued in occupation, with one break, into the 160s. Thereafter the nature of the military presence changed. Two compounds were constructed in the southern part of what had been the fort (they were later amalgamated into one), while the granaries were rebuilt and continued in use. Around this military core grew a town which at one time extended to 30 acres (12 hectares). The importance of Corbridge sprang from its position at the junction of the Stanegate, which ran westwards to Carlisle and Dere Street, leading northwards into Scotland and southward to London. It was also, until the

construction of Hadrian's bridge over the Tyne at Newcastle, the lowest crossing-point on the river.

In the centre of the town lay an impressive fountain and a group of temples, which have produced some remarkable sculpture. Gods from the Orient as well as local deities were worshipped here. All this reflects the cosmopolitan nature of this town on the very edge of the Roman world.

Also in the heart of the town lies a levelled area on which a large courtyard building was erected. Construction of this vast building ended abruptly in the late second century, perhaps in the early 180s when the northern tribes are known to have invaded the province.

© CROWN COPYRIGHT, NMR

TOUR OF CORBRIDGE ROMAN FORT *(Coria)*

The **museum** should be the first stop. On leaving here, turn right along the side of the granaries and then left on to the **Stanegate**. This road was in use for over 300 years so it is not surprising that many resurfacings raised its level above the surrounding buildings. The two **granaries** had stone floors supported on low walls. This was to help keep the food dry and fresh. The side vents in the walls were partially closed by mullions; one survives in the east wall of the east granary. A porch over each entrance was supported by the columns on the road side. The right granary retains its loading bay.

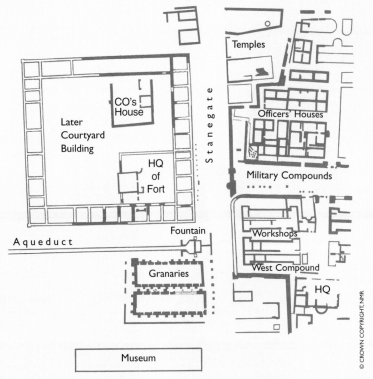

LEFT: This base and tank are all that survive of an ornamental fountain, once embellished with statues and sculpture. Behind can be seen the base of the aqueduct which brought water to the fountain

BELOW: Aerial view of Corbridge Roman site, looking east. The undulations across the southern side of the site are caused by differential subsidence over the roads and buildings of the earlier forts, the roads having prevented subsidence

Continue along the Stanegate to the **fountain**, with its great water tank in front, fed by an aqueduct, the base for which can be seen leading away behind. A section of the channel survives further north. Below the front of the water tank are the remains of an earlier military building. Walk on to view the great unfinished **courtyard building** (Site XI). Within it lie (left) the headquarters building and (right) the commanding officer's house of an earlier fort. Continue on to the end of the road, passing the remains of **temples** to the right, and turn right to look at the reconstruction drawing of the site. Walk on along the fence and turn right to pass across the site, through the military compounds, passing the officers' houses, to the **headquarters building** of the west compound, in which there is a strong room.

ABOVE: Pottery appliqué figure of a smith god

RIGHT: Bronze jug

Because it was unfinished it is difficult now to determine its original purpose, and suggestions include a storehouse, a legionary headquarters building and the forum for a new town. Within the courtyard lie some remains of the earlier forts, the headquarters building and the commanding officer's house.

Corbridge was occupied until the end of Roman Britain in the early fifth century. It was one of the earliest Roman sites to be 'excavated', for under King John looters came to seek buried treasure. Modern excavation began in 1906 and continued into the 1970s.

BELOW: A view looking along the west side of the unfinished courtyard building, which overlies the remains of the earlier headquarters building. The uncompleted state of the courtyard building is shown by the walls; many stones were only partly dressed by the masons before abandonment. The south range of the building was later converted into shops

BOTTOM: The strong room in the headquarters building of the west compound

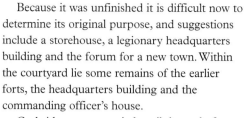

ABOVE: A sculpture of Hercules killing the Hydra (on the missing piece of the stone), aided by Athena (left). This was found in the central room, the shrine, of the headquarters of the west compound. The god Hercules was particularly favoured by soldiers

LEFT: The only surviving mullion in a granary ventilator slot in Britain is in the east granary at Corbridge

BELOW: The east granary looking north. The walls are supported by buttresses; narrow gaps in the walls allowed cool air to enter and circulate below the stone floors of the granaries. The roof was probably originally of tile

ABOVE RIGHT: Pottery lamp in lead lamp holder

RIGHT: This depiction of the Sun god probably once adorned a temple to Dolichenus

ABOVE: An altar to Jupiter Dolichenus, Caelestis-Brigantia and Salus, dedicated by a centurion of legion VI Victrix. This altar illustrates the all-embracing nature of Roman religion. The Roman god Jupiter is identified with the eastern deity Dolichenus, and associated with the personification of the local tribe the Brigantes, who is perceived as a local manifestation of Juno Caelestis, the consort of Jupiter Dolichenus, from either Africa or Syria. The final deity is Salus, the god of personal wellbeing

© CROWN COPYRIGHT, NMR

29

Sewingshields Carrawburgh
Housesteads Chesters
Willowford Cawfields Brunton Turret
Birdoswald Walltown Vindolanda Corbridge Roman Town
Bowness-on-Solway CARLISLE Heddon-on-the-Wall NEWCASTLE UPON TYNE South Shields Roman Fort Wallsend

© CROWN COPYRIGHT, NMR

THE CHESTERS AREA

FAR RIGHT: Brunton turret (26b)

FAR RIGHT BELOW: Here, at Planetrees, the Wall was reduced in thickness from ten to six Roman feet. This would have reduced the workload of the legionaries and might have been ordered for that reason

BELOW: Chesters bridge abutment. The earlier pier can be discerned to the left, within the masonry of the abutment of the later bridge. The tower probably provided access to this later bridge. To the right of the tower are the cover slabs of a water channel probably leading to a mill. Along the front edge, and running back, are grooves which once held tie rods to keep the bridge firm against the force of the river

BOTTOM: Reconstruction drawing of the Chesters bridge

Across the river from Chesters fort lies the east abutment of the bridge over the river North Tyne. A pier embedded in this abutment probably formed part of the Hadrianic bridge. This is thought to have had ten stone piers supporting a timber superstructure carrying a walk across the river. The position of the robbed east abutment of the bridge and a section of the paved riverbed can be seen in the bottom of the later tower.

The visible abutment, built in the later second century, encompassed the first pier of its predecessor. A gate tower, the basement of which survives, probably gave access to a bridge consisting of three stone arches. Many carved stones from the superstructure of this bridge remain on the site. In the later Roman period a water channel, probably serving a mill south of the bridge, was led through the tower basement.

Eastwards from Chesters Bridge and a few yards from the modern road lies Brunton turret (26b). This still stands nearly 8 ft (2.4 m) high. From its western side runs the Wall built to the original specification, 10 Roman feet thick. On the east side a

much narrower Wall, about 6 ft (2 m) thick, rides up over the turret's wing wall. The differences probably result from changes in plan during construction of the Wall.

Half a mile to the east of Brunton turret a short length of Wall lies at Planetrees. Here there is another point where the Wall was reduced from the original 10 Roman feet, in this case to about 6 feet. It is clear that the soldiers laying the Wall's foundations had progressed quicker than the builders of the superstructure as the foundations continue on past the point of reduction. Interestingly, the foundation builders also appear to have laid the drain, most of which is incorporated into the narrow wall. West of Chesters a mile length of Wall climbing up to Limestone Corner contains a turret at Black Carts (29a). This turret seems to have continued in occupation into the fourth century.

30

Sewingshields Carrawburgh
Housesteads
Willowford Cawfields
Birdoswald   Chesters
                                    Brunton
Walltown Vindolanda   Turret
Heddon-on-   NEWCASTLE   South Shields
the-Wall   UPON TYNE   Roman Fort
Bowness-on-Solway   Corbridge
CARLISLE   Roman Town
                                    Wallsend

CHESTERS *(Cilurnum)* ROMAN FORT

Chesters fort lies in the pleasant valley of the River North Tyne. Here, in the parkland laid out by the Clayton family in the early nineteenth century, can be viewed remains of the fort, the well-preserved bath house and the remarkable museum built 80 years ago to house the great collection brought together by John Clayton.

An inscription found as recently as 1978 demonstrated that Chesters was built for *ala Augusta ob virtutem appellata*, a cavalry regiment 'called Augusta for valour'. Other units are attested at the fort in the second century, but from the end of the century Chesters was the base for the Second Cavalry Regiment of Asturians (originally raised in Spain), which remained here for 200 years.

Chesters was built astride the Wall with three of its four main gates opening north of the Wall. Access south of the Wall was increased by the provision of an extra pair of side gates. The circuit of defences, only part of which can be seen, was strengthened by the provision of towers at the four corners of the fort and at intervals along the walls. One or two ditches, now silted up, lay beyond the fort wall. Outside the fort was the bath house, one of the best preserved buildings of Roman Britain, and a civil settlement, which has not been excavated.

Statue of the goddess Juno Dolichena standing on a heifer

A reconstruction drawing by Alan Sorrell of the fort and civil settlement at Chesters

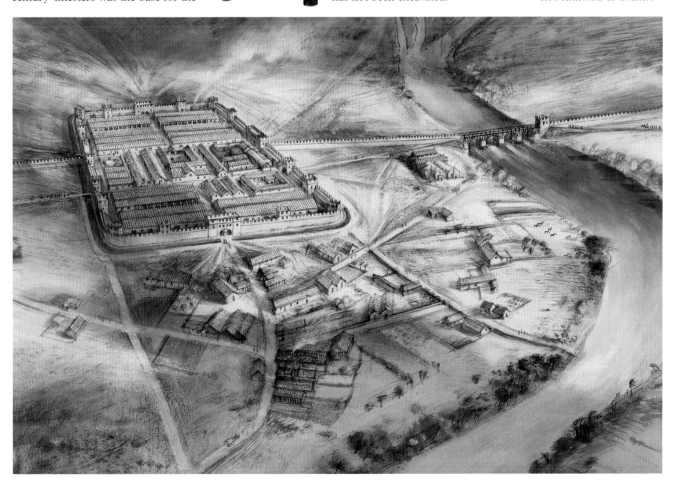

TOUR OF CHESTERS

On leaving the ticket office, turn left along the path to the fort. Ahead lies the **north gate**. Two roadways passed through this gate. A drain exited the fort below the west (right) road. Turn right towards the **west gate**. Here the iron collars which formerly held the door pivots can be seen. A water channel leads into the north (right) guard chamber, and beyond it is an oven. Hadrian's Wall abuts the south (left) guard chamber. Continue on round the perimeter of the fort past an interval tower to the **south gate**. This shows much evidence of use; the road was finally raised 30 in (800 mm) above the Hadrianic level. Another interval tower lies beyond the gate. Turn left at the angle tower and walk to the **minor east gate**, noting, to the left, the columns of a barrack block verandah. Leave the fort here and turn right down to the **bath house**.

The **bath house** is a complex building, rendered more difficult to understand by the lack of floors in the heated rooms. Pass through the **porch** into the **changing room**; the function of the seven niches is uncertain. To the left is the **latrine**, ahead the door leading into the heated rooms. To the right of the first room, a vestibule, are the two rooms of the **hot dry suite** (some of the flags are modern). Note the stone door jambs (wood would have warped) and the furnace outside the room. To the left of the vestibule lay the **cold room** containing a basin for cold water and, ahead, a cold bath later replaced by the smaller cold bath to the left. A cold bath was necessary to close the pores before leaving the bath house.

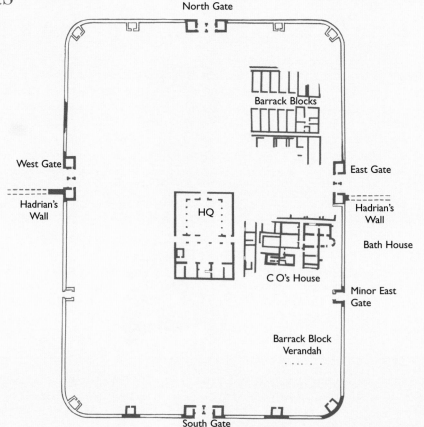

© CROWN COPYRIGHT, NMR

Beyond the vestibule is the **steam range**. The floors have been removed so today we walk around in the basement. The first room, formerly two, was the hottest and therefore last in the sequence; the two warm rooms to the left were entered first by the bather. At the far end of the hot room lies the furnace, where the boiler formerly sat (at one time this may have served as a hot bath). To the right is the hot bath with a window above;

ABOVE RIGHT: The barrack blocks today. The drain would have been covered by stone slabs

RIGHT: Reconstruction by Peter Connolly of a pair of facing barrack blocks at Chesters fort

AIRFOTOS LTD, NEWCASTLE

ABOVE: Aerial view of Chesters looking north. The headquarters building lies in the centre of the fort with the commanding officer's house to the right. Parts of the three barrack blocks lie to the upper right. To the right, outside the fort, is the bath house

© CROWN COPYRIGHT, NMR

Hadrian's Wall, one pier still standing at the beginning of the arch. Pass through the gate, go round to the right and step over the wall into the centurion's suite of the **barrack block**. Walk through this and along the road between the two barrack blocks. The individual rooms, each thought to have been occupied by eight soldiers, were probably divided into two by timber partitions.

Outside the modern gate to this enclosure, turn left and, bearing right, cross the field to enter the **headquarters building**. The large courtyard is surrounded by a colonnade; possibly notices were pinned up here. Beside the well, on the paving, is a phallic symbol, a good-luck charm. Continue into the assembly hall, with its dais or tribunal to the right, now reduced to its lowest courses. Beyond, the back rooms are well preserved. The two to the right were probably used by the clerks of the regimental office, and the two to the left by the accounts clerks. In the centre was the unit's shrine, where a statue of the emperor and the regiment's standards would have been placed. Leading off this is the strong room; when opened up in the early nineteenth century, its oak door disintegrated on exposure to the air.

Leave the headquarters building by the side entrance and examine the **commanding officer's house**. The present maze of rooms is the result of additions and rebuildings over many years; a small bath house lies at the far end.

Return from here to the **museum**. This was opened in 1903 and has been little altered since that date. It contains many finds from Chesters and other forts on Hadrian's Wall once owned by the Clayton family.

note the plaster on the wall beside the bath. Before leaving, walk round the back of the bath house to see the voussoirs (wedge-shaped stones) from the barrel-vaulted ceiling; these are made from a lightweight rock called tufa.

Beyond the fort are slight remains of the west abutment of the bridge (see page 30). Return to the fort and enter the **east gate**. This is one of the most impressive gates on

ABOVE LEFT: A reconstruction by Alan Sorrell of the assembly hall with the tribunal to the right, and the back rooms in the headquarters building

LEFT: The headquarters building. In the foreground is the courtyard and beyond it the assembly hall and the back rooms

ABOVE: Statue of a river god, possibly Neptune, found in the commanding officer's bath house at Chesters

ABOVE RIGHT: The strong room at Chesters. Here the regiment's money was kept. Access was from the adjacent shrine in the foreground, where a guard was on duty at all times

RIGHT: The commanding officer's bath house, showing the furnace and the raised floor of the hot room behind

BELOW: The fort bath house at Chesters, looking across the changing room to the steam range. The niches to the right many have been for clothes or small statues; the arches were probably originally window heads

© CROWN COPYRIGHT, NMR

Bowness-on-Solway · CARLISLE · Birdoswald · Willowford · Cawfields · Walltown · Housesteads · Sewingshields · Vindolanda · Carrawburgh · Chesters · Brunton Turret · Corbridge Roman Town · Heddon-on-the-Wall · NEWCASTLE UPON TYNE · South Shields Roman Fort · Wallsend

CARRAWBURGH *(Brocolitia)*: TEMPLE TO MITHRAS

The fort is in private ownership, but English Heritage looks after an area around it that includes a remarkable temple to the god Mithras. The fort was an addition to the Wall, probably being built in the 130s. By this time, the Vallum had been constructed and its ditch had to be filled, and its mounds levelled, when the fort was built over it. In the third and fourth centuries Carrawburgh was the home of the First Cohort of Batavians, a regiment originally raised from a tribe living at the mouth of the Rhine. The mithraeum (temple to Mithras) was probably constructed by soldiers based in the fort; the three altars found here (copies stand in the temple) were all dedicated by commanding officers of the unit. Mithras was an Eastern god. According to legend, he had captured and killed in a cave the primeval bull, the first creature created on earth, and from this slaying sprang the benefits of mankind. So mithraea were dark and gloomy, purposefully resembling caves. Mithras was supported by his attendants, Cautes and Cautopates.

Mithraism was especially disliked by Christians, who saw in the mithraic ritual of taking bread and water a caricature of their own holy sacrament. Thus it may have been Christians rather than barbarians who destroyed

TOUR

The mithraeum at Carrawburgh had been buried under peat for over 1600 years before its rediscovery in 1949

From the car park, follow the path round the side of the fort.

In front of the mithraeum, one slab of the water tank of the shrine of the Nymphs sticks out of the turf. Inside the door of the mithraeum is an ante-chapel. This would have been used for the initiation tests, which worshippers had to pass before being allowed to proceed to the next grade in the temple hierarchy (there were seven grades: Raven, Bridegroom, Soldier, Lion, Persian, Courier of the Sun and Father). In the right-hand corner is a small statue of a mother goddess. This is a copy, like the other statues and the altars and also the timber posts and wattles. To the left is a hearth, used for ordeals or preparing ritual feasts.

Cautes and Cautopates guard the nave. Here benches lie on either side of a central passage. Worshippers would have reclined on these benches during ceremonies.

At the far end of the temple is the sanctuary containing the altars. On one altar Mithras appears as the Charioteer of the Sun; this stone has been hollowed out behind so that a lamp placed in the receptacle will cause the rays to light up. Above the altars, resting on the projecting stone, would have been a sculpture of Mithras killing the bull. The original altars and sculptures are in the Museum of Antiquities, Newcastle.

MUSEUM OF ANTIQUITIES, NEWCASTLE

this temple in the fourth century, smashing the reredos, the scene depicting Mithras killing the bull, but leaving intact the altars dedicated by commanding officers.

North of the mithraeum is Coventina's Well (not in the care of English Heritage). A pool on the site of the sacred spring is all that survives of this temple to the water goddess Coventina. 13,490 coins were found here when the temple was examined in 1876, as well as inscriptions, sculptures, pottery vessels, incense burners and brooches, all thrown in to honour, or help win favours from the goddess. Many of these objects can be seen at Chesters Museum.

LEFT: This full-scale reconstruction of the Carrawburgh mithraeum is in the Museum of Antiquities, Newcastle upon Tyne. It reminds us that Roman buildings and sculptures, now so drab, were once brightly painted. Cautes and Cautopates flank the nave, while above the altars is the tauroctomy, the scene of Mithras killing the bull

35

Bowness-on-Solway
CARLISLE
Birdoswald
Willowford Cawfields
Walltown
Sewingshields
Housesteads
Carrawburgh
Vindolanda
Chesters
Brunton
Turret
Corbridge
Roman Town
Heddon-on-
the-Wall
NEWCASTLE
UPON TYNE
South Shields
Roman Fort
Wallsend

SEWINGSHIELDS TO HOUSESTEADS

*FAR RIGHT, ABOVE: Turret
34a has very short wing walls.
Part of the wall blocking the
internal recess has been
removed to reveal the original
north wall of the turret.
Beside the blocking wall is a
platform. Possibly this was
where the soldiers slept*

*FAR RIGHT, BELOW: Turret
33b looking east. This turret
went out of use in the later
second century. At first the
door was blocked up and then
the turret was demolished
down to the bottom four
courses and the recess on the
north side blocked up, perhaps
to eliminate the resulting
weak point in the Wall, or to
allow a walk along the top
of the Wall to be carried
across the site of the turret*

*ABOVE: The Vallum at
Sewingshields. The modern
road drops dramatically into
the Vallum ditch. Set back
on either side of the ditch is
a mound: on the south lip
an extra mound is probably
the result of later cleaning
out of the ditch*

*RIGHT: An aerial view of
milecastle 35 and the Wall
from the west. The recently
excavated milecastle is
perched on the very edge of
the crag: a north gate was
clearly superfluous here*

Two miles of Hadrian's Wall between
Sewingshields and Housesteads are in the care
of English Heritage and another mile is owned
by the National Trust. This sector is best reached
from Housesteads. Although perhaps less
spectacular than the crags to the west, it contains
many interesting features and there are
magnificent views north, south and westwards
to Housesteads, Cuddy's Crags and beyond.

At the eastern end of this stretch is turret 33b.
During excavation, an inscription recording the
Sixth Legion was found built into one of its
walls. This turret, together with the other two
visible in this stretch, 34a and 35a, were all
abandoned in the later second century. Just
short of turret 34a, as the Wall moves up onto
the crags, the ditch stops with a neatly rounded-
off end.

Milecastle 35 was excavated between 1978
and 1980. There is now no north gate to this
milecastle, but the rebuilt north wall has
destroyed any evidence that may have existed for
a gate in the Hadrianic period. The original
barrack accommodation in the south-east corner
of the milecastle is overlain by its early third-
century successor. The jumble of walls in the

western half of the milecastle belongs to the
third- and fourth-century buildings. The site was
reoccupied in the Middle Ages
when a farm was built here.
Several short lengths of Wall
are visible between milecastle
35 and turret 35a. In places,
the foundations are as wide
as 11 Roman feet, though
the Wall itself, built after the
decision to narrow it, is
usually about 8 feet wide.
One stretch is particularly
interesting for, in a dip, the
Wall is stepped down on one
side, while riding with the
contours on the other. Below
the north-east corner of
Housesteads fort is the Knag
Burn gate, which was
probably inserted into the
Wall in the fourth century.

Bowness-on-Solway / CARLISLE · Birdoswald · Willowford · Cawfields · Sewingshields · Housesteads · Walltown · Vindolanda · Carrawburgh · Chesters · Brunton Turret · Corbridge Roman Town · Heddon-on-the-Wall · NEWCASTLE UPON TYNE · South Shields Roman Fort · Wallsend

HOUSESTEADS (*Vercovicium*) ROMAN FORT

Housesteads is the best-known fort on Hadrian's Wall. This is as it should be, for the fort, perched high on its ridge overlooking the Northumbrian countryside, conveys the spirit of the past as well as the beauty of the present.

The fort at Housesteads was an addition to Hadrian's Wall, forming part of the second scheme for the frontier. When it was built, a turret, erected a short time before on the site, was demolished. In order to gain as much room as possible on the ridge, the north wall of the fort was pushed to the very edge of the escarpment. This entailed building deep foundations for the fort wall, and these can still be seen below the threshold of the north gate, though they would once have been covered by a ramp.

Housesteads fort covers 5 acres (2 hectares) and was occupied through the third and fourth centuries by the First Cohort of Tungrians, a unit that had originally been raised from one of the tribes of present-day Belgium. This was an infantry regiment nominally 1000 strong, though in practice it probably only contained 800. The fort was probably built for a similar sized unit. In the third century, the Cohort of Tungrians was strengthened by two other units, Notfried's regiment from Germany, and a unit of Frisians raised from the tribe that lived at the mouth of the River Rhine. Today the buildings exposed are of different periods, reflecting the long and complex history of the site, although the overall layout changed little over the nearly three centuries of occupation.

The fort at Housesteads lay at the centre of a thriving community. All that can now be seen of this civil settlement is the small group of buildings that are on view outside the south gate of the fort. These buildings probably included shops, inns and, furthest from the fort, a house where, it appears, a murder had been committed and the bodies buried beneath the floor.

This sculpture of Victory once adorned the east gate

This reconstruction shows Housesteads as it might have looked in the third century when the civil settlement had spread over the slopes south of the fort

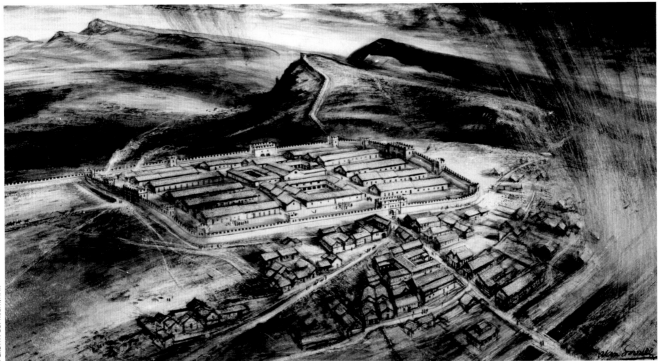

© CROWN COPYRIGHT, NMR

TOUR OF HOUSESTEADS ROMAN FORT *(Vercovicium)*

Go first to the **museum**. Here is a display of finds from the site and a model of the fort and civil settlement. On leaving the museum, head for the entrance to the fort. Walk along the inside of the fort wall to the **south gate**. Its eastern guard chamber was extended and the kiln inserted when border raiders lived here in the seventeenth century. From the gate observe the buildings of the **civil settlement** beyond. Notice how the front walls of these buildings line up with the centre of the gate, not the far side, demonstrating that the far (east) portal of the gate had been blocked by the time the houses were built in the third century. Continue along the inside of the south wall to the **latrine**. Wooden seats would have covered the main sewer channel, which was fed with water from the adjacent tanks. The small channel was used for washing the sponges used instead of toilet paper.

Proceed on round the fort to the **east gate** – the front gate of the fort. The southern passage of the gate was completely blocked up at some stage in its history and the guard chamber turned into a coal store. The deeply worn wheel-ruts are about 4 ft 8 in (1.4 m) apart. This is the normal width of cart axles from antiquity to the present day, and is reflected by the standard railway gauge of 4 ft 8½ in. Continue on a little way and turn left to pass between the two fourth-century **barrack blocks**, each built as a series of separate buildings. At the far end, to the right, lies the **north**

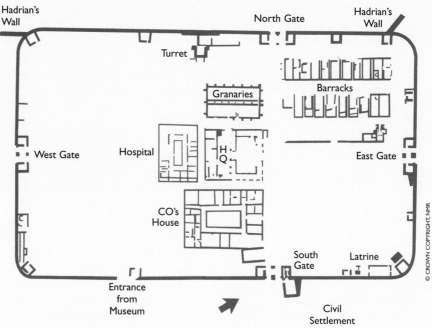

gate, and beyond it the **turret** demolished when the fort was built; this is now partly obscured by the walls of later buildings.

At the turret, turn left to the **granaries**. The first is the best preserved and details of its door (bolted on the inside), stone supports for the floor and ventilator holes in the walls can be examined. Walk on to the corner of the second granary. Ahead lie two buildings, the **hospital** to the right (this consists of wards and a large room to the north, interpreted as an operating theatre, all ranged round a courtyard) and the **headquarters building** to the left. Immediately before you are the rooms where regimental clerks worked and where the standards of the unit were housed (the two far rooms have been modified by the insertion of a staircase at the rear). Enter the building by the steps to your left and note the commanding officer's dais on

your right facing down the assembly hall. Pass, left, through the courtyard and turn right down the main street of the fort to the **commanding officer's house**, again a series of rooms round an open courtyard. To the right lies the kitchen containing an oven; the dining room presumably lay near here. The heated room in the centre of the north range served as a bath suite for a time. A latrine, and its later replacement, lay in the centre of the west range. The basements beside the entrance served as stables.

After viewing the buildings in the central range of the fort, walk to the **west gate** (back gate) of the fort. This preserves two interesting features: the holes for the bar that was slotted into place when the gate was closed and, by the front corners of the gate, the marking out lines scored by the masons who built it. It is a short walk from here to Housesteads milecastle.

LEFT: *Aerial view of Housesteads looking south. The characteristic playing card shape of the fort is clear. Within lay 18 buildings. Visible now are the headquarters building in the centre, the granaries in the foreground, the commanding officer's house beyond and the hospital to the right. Bottom left are two barrack blocks and a storehouse. Outside the fort, part of the civil settlement is visible*

BELOW: *The headquarters building looking south-west. The assembly hall in the centre is flanked on the left by the courtyard, and on the right by the rooms for the administrative staff*

On the hillside below the civil settlement is a series of terraces. These were originally long, thin fields, but it is uncertain whether they are Roman or later in date. Certain other features at Housesteads reflect later occupation. The additions to the south gate and the corn-drying kilns here and in the granaries were all in use at the time Housesteads was the base for border raiders in the seventeenth century. More recently, farming has left its traces, for example in the round enclosure before the museum, which surrounds a well.

RIGHT: *This sculpture of Mars was once placed over the entrance to the head-quarters building*

LEFT: *The communal latrine in the south-east corner of the fort. A complex arrangement of tanks and channels ensured the supply of water to this building, and a main drain carried the sewerage out of the fort. The wooden seats over the sewer channel have long since rotted, but the joist holes remain. The latrine and the hospital emphasize the Roman army's care for hygiene and health*

RIGHT: Food of all kinds was stored in the granaries on a raised floor supported on stone pillars. Ventilating slots in the wall helped air to circulate below the floor and keep it fresh. The two granaries were probably originally one large building with a colonnade down the centre

© CROWN COPYRIGHT, NMR

BELOW: A reconstruction of the granaries by Peter Connolly. The soldier carries a sack, which we know was used in Roman times. The grain may have been stored inside the granary in bins or in sacks

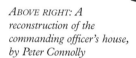

ABOVE RIGHT: A reconstruction of the commanding officer's house, by Peter Connolly

ABOVE: View of the west gate

RIGHT: The commanding officer's house consisted of a range of rooms round an open courtyard. It was a large house, as befitted the commander's status, and provided accommodation for himself, his family and his slaves. In the foreground lies the kitchen containing the ovens

HOUSESTEADS TO STEEL RIGG

The three-mile stretch of Hadrian's Wall from the fort at Housesteads over Cuddy's Crags, Hotbank Crags and Peel Crags to Steel Rigg is the most spectacular section of the whole Wall. It is owned by the National Trust. There is a splendid, strenuous walk between Housesteads and Steel Rigg car park. This can be started at either end, but for convenience it is described from east (Housesteads) to west.

A short walk of less than half a mile along the top of the Wall leads to milecastle 37. This is one of the best-preserved milecastles on the Wall. Part of an inscription found here demonstrates that it was built by the Second Legion. The gates were built of the large stones, which are the hallmark of this legion's work at milecastles. The north gate here is particularly well preserved. The east half of the milecastle is occupied by a stone-built barrack block; the back wall of the building has been destroyed. This barrack is large enough to have housed eight men. Those visitors not wishing to continue to Steel Rigg can return to the fort along the path that follows the Military Way south of the Wall.

The Wall strides on from Housesteads milecastle over Cuddy's Crags. John Clayton of Chesters was responsible for the clearing of this stretch of Wall from its accumulated debris in the nineteenth century.

Along the south face can be seen many junctions where presumably different building gangs met. Other aspects of construction are interesting. On a gentle slope, for example, the courses follow the contours. When the slope steepens the courses are laid horizontally and the Wall stepped down the hill. No ditch is necessary along most of this sector, but it reappears on the low ground at Hotbank and again at Steel Rigg.

One Roman mile west of Housesteads milecastle lie the hollows which marked the robbed-out walls of Hotbank milecastle. Two inscriptions of the Second Legion have been found here, one fallen from the north gate, the other from the south. It can be seen that there is no break in the ditch in front of the north gate. A few yards walk south along the track leads to the ruins of the native farmstead of Milking Gap (to the right of the track).

The Wall runs on along the crags overlooking Crags Lough. A particularly fine stretch by Highshields Crags survives to a height of 10 feet. The next milecastle sits in Castle Nick. This is not the same type of milecastle as those at Housesteads (37) and Hotbank (38); in fact it is the only milecastle of this particular type to be seen on Hadrian's Wall and was probably built by the Sixth Legion. The gates are not as originally constructed, having been later modified.

The last stretch of the Wall before the car park at Steel Rigg runs along Peel Crags. Here lies an extra tower, only discovered in 1987. Beyond the car park and across the road is the highest point on the Wall at Winshields Crags. The earthworks of the unexcavated milecastle 40 may be viewed here. Part of this length of the Wall is owned by the National Trust; the rest is in the care of English Heritage.

ABOVE: Milecastle 37 (Housesteads). Several of the arch stones survive at the north gate

BELOW: Milecastle 39 (Castle Nick) looking north-west. Occupation of this milecastle continued into the late fourth century

BELOW: Aerial view of Hadrian's Wall looking east from Hotbank Crags

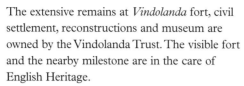

CHESTERHOLM *(Vindolanda)*

VINDOLANDA TRUST

FAR RIGHT: The apsidal building in the courtyard of the commanding officer's house, interpreted as a Christian church

BELOW: The headquarters building. The front panel would have been balanced by a second on the other side of the entrance to the office

The extensive remains at *Vindolanda* fort, civil settlement, reconstructions and museum are owned by the Vindolanda Trust. The visible fort and the nearby milestone are in the care of English Heritage.

There were several forts at *Vindolanda* before Hadrian's Wall was built. These are not visible, being buried deep below the later fort and its civil settlement. When Hadrian's Wall was built, a new fort appears to have been constructed at *Vindolanda*. In the early third century this was rebuilt and troops continued to be based here into the early fifth century. The garrison during the third and fourth centuries was the Fourth Cohort of Gauls, a mixed infantry and cavalry regiment originally raised in what is now France.

The civil settlement is the most extensive such site to be seen on Hadrian's Wall, and indeed anywhere in Britain. Here are exposed the lower courses of houses and shops, a building thought to be an official rest house for the imperial post *(mansio)* and the regiment's bath house; an earlier bath house lies outside the fort's south gate. There are also two burial tombs visible beside the reconstructions. The civil settlement was first built in the middle of the second century and it continued in occupation, with a short break, until the late third century. Parts of the settlement appear to have been reoccupied in the late fourth century.

RIGHT: Vindolanda from the air looking north. The fort lies to the right. The civil settlement straddles the road leading out of the left (west) gate; the bath house lies to the right of the road

BELOW: Helmet plume found at Vindolanda

TOUR OF CHESTERHOLM *(Vindolanda)*

Visitors will probably approach the site along the Stanegate, arriving at the western car park. A joint admission ticket is available. A visit to the **reconstructions**, passing the **wells** on the right, is recommended first. Here is a section of stone wall with turret and ditch, a length of turf wall and ditch and a timber milecastle gate.

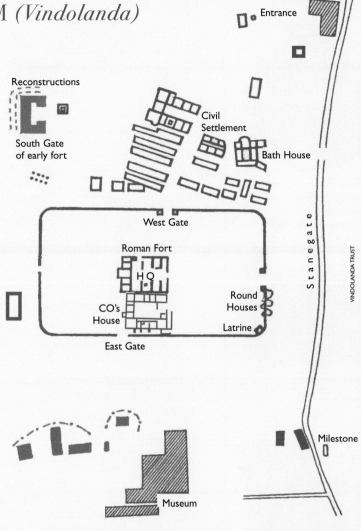

A full-scale reconstruction of a turret and length of Wall at Vindolanda

Return past the **burial tombs** to the main path and the **civil settlement**. The buildings here were first constructed in the mid-second century. Visit the *mansio* with its rooms, kitchen, bath house (back left) and latrine, round an open courtyard. Across the road lies a large **house** with three rooms on either side of a corridor. This was later divided into two houses. Behind this lies the unit's **bath house**, which still retains some of its original wall-plaster. Return to the main path and walk along the road to the fort. The houses here approach close to the fort wall, being built over the filled-in fort ditches in the third century.

Enter the **fort** at the **west gate**, which has only one passageway flanked by towers. Cross to the **headquarters building**. This follows the normal design, except that the front verandah and the courtyard aisles served as storehouses, while small rooms were added to the rear of the back rooms. There is no strong room, but a pit was provided to house the money chests. To the east of the headquarters is the **commanding officer's house**, recently excavated and consolidated. This is the normal courtyard house, but with the unique distinction of

containing a small apsidal building, interpreted as a church. Behind these buildings lies the **south gate**. Immediately outside the gate is the first-century **bath house**. To the right lie some round structures, possibly houses, destroyed by the construction of the fort wall.

Cross to the **north gate**. To the right lie further round buildings and, in the north-east corner of the fort, the **latrine**. Walk on along the east wall, out of the east gate (which unusually has no flanking towers), and down to the **museum**, noting the well-preserved fort wall.

This Roman milestone on the Stanegate still stands where it was originally erected

VINDOLANDA TRUST

FINDS FROM *VINDOLANDA*

This betrothal medallion is a rare find in Britain. Made of Whitby jet, it was probably carved in York

A cloth fragment from the pre-Hadrianic fort

A child's sock

THE *VINDOLANDA* WRITING TABLETS

The unearthing of the first wooden writing tablet at *Vindolanda* 30 years ago heralded one of the most important archaeological discoveries in Britain since 1945. The cache of about 2000 documents is an invaluable source of information about life in the Roman army on the northern frontier in the years immediately before the construction of Hadrian's Wall. The tablets are so similar in many ways to documents found on the eastern frontier of the empire that they allow that material to be used with confidence to illuminate life in Roman Britain.

The *Vindolanda* writing tablets include letters from senior officers and their wives, reports of military activities, lists, communications concerning food, clothing and other supplies, building and transport. They provide evidence for local place-names as well as the administration of justice. They even give the price of beer!

RIGHT: This writing tablet contains a commentary on the fighting tactics of the Britons: 'The cavalry does not use swords, nor do the wretched Britons mount in order to throw javelins.'

ABOVE: This fragment of a letter, written in pen and ink on a wooden writing tablet records the sending of socks, sandals and underpants, probably to a soldier stationed at Vindolanda

LEFT: On 11 September about the year 100, Lepidius, wife of the commanding officer at Vindolanda, received this invitation to celebrate the birthday of Claudia Severa. This is almost certainly the earliest known example of a woman's handwriting in Latin

This glass gladiator cup shows two umpires, a heavily armed secutor *and the* retiarius *with his net and trident*

BELOW: Many leather shoes have been found in the civil settlement. This is a lady's slipper, stamped with the maker's name, L. AEB. THALES T. F: Lucius Aebutius Thales, son of Titus

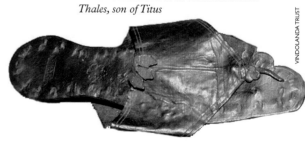

Sewingshields Carrawburgh
Housesteads
Willowford Cawfields   Chesters
Birdoswald   Brunton
Walltown Vindolanda   Turret
                          Corbridge
                          Roman Town
owness-on-Solway
CARLISLE

Heddon-on- South Shields
the-Wall NEWCASTLE Roman Fort
UPON TYNE
Wallsend

CAWFIELDS TO WALLTOWN

The milecastle at Cawfields sits awkwardly on the hillside, cut off to the west by the raw edge of a modern quarry. It was excavated nearly 150 years ago by John Clayton of Chesters. Today it is hard to imagine how the internal buildings could have been arranged sensibly within it, and no trace of any has survived. The massive masonry of the gates has yielded an inscription recording that the milecastle was built by the Second Legion.

A dramatic stretch of Wall runs eastwards from the milecastle for two-thirds of a Roman mile past Thorny Doors. Here is one of the highest standing sections of Hadrian's Wall. A little further on is turret 41a, demolished in the late second century.

Three miles west of Cawfields, the Wall snakes over Walltown Crags. Here again the modern topography has been altered by quarrying, thus chopping the Wall into short stretches. On the steep slope of Mucklebank Crag lies turret 44b, its view obscured to the east by the hill on which it sits, but with an impressive vista to the west. A little further on is turret 45a, originally built as a freestanding tower. At the west end of Walltown Crags, beside the fort at Carvoran, is the Roman Army Museum.

ABOVE: A most impressive stretch of Wall climbs over Walltown Crags

FAR LEFT: The Wall and Vallum at Cawfields looking east. Both mounds of the Vallum can be observed, symmetrically placed on either side of the ditch

LEFT: Turret 45a was built as a freestanding tower before the Wall. It probably served as a lookout post in advance of the forts on the Stanegate

BELOW: Cawfields milecastle (42) hanging on the hillside on this dramatic stretch of the Wall

AIRFOTOS LTD, NEWCASTLE

GILSLAND TO WILLOWFORD

Here is one of the most instructive miles on the whole line of the Wall. This is the only mile where the milecastles at both ends and the two turrets in between can be seen, as well as much of the Wall itself.

At the eastern end sits Poltross Burn milecastle (48). This is larger than usual and it contains two barrack blocks, one on either side of a central road. The gates are different from those visible at Housesteads and Cawfields milecastles (37 and 42), for example, and suggest that it was built by a different legion. Like several other milecastles, its north gate was narrowed in later years.

Across the railway in the grounds of the former vicarage garden lies the next stretch of Wall. Here the building of the Wall to its original width of 10 Roman feet was never completed, and a narrower wall sits on top of a broad base. The modern road has to be crossed to reach the next sector and from here the Wall runs down to the River Irthing and Willowford Bridge. Throughout this length, narrow wall usually sits on the uncompleted broad wall. At Poltross Burn milecastle and at the two turrets (48a and 48b) it can be seen that these structures also were

completed, with wing walls, at least to their present height, before the Wall was narrowed. At the far end of this sector is Willowford Bridge, again built earlier than the narrow wall, as indicated by a short length of original broad wall obscured by a later tower on the south side of the bridge. The river has moved westwards since the Roman period, leaving the bridge on dry land. It also moved during the Roman period, and as a result the bridge itself had to be extended westwards. Above the remains of the bridge on the bank of the river sits Harrow's Scar milecastle (49), which can be reached from the footbridge over the river.

ABOVE: To the right of the north gate of Poltross Burn milecastle (48), a few steps remain of what was presumably a staircase leading to the top of the Wall. These steps allow the height of the milecastle wall, and possibly therefore Hadrian's Wall itself, to be calculated as 15 ft (4.3 m) on the north side

RIGHT: Milecastle 48 (Poltross Burn) from the air. Each of the two barrack blocks was originally divided into four rooms, perhaps accommodating 32 men

BELOW: Willowford east turret (48a)

RIGHT: Harrow's Scar milecastle (49) sits above the River Irthing to the left, while to the right the remains of Willowford Bridge now lie in a field, owing to the movement of the river

Map showing Hadrian's Wall sites: Bowness-on-Solway, CARLISLE, Birdoswald, Walltown, Cawfields, Vindolanda, Housesteads, Sewingshields, Carrawburgh, Chesters, Brunton Turret, Corbridge Roman Town, Heddon-on-the-Wall, NEWCASTLE UPON TYNE, South Shields Roman Fort, Wallsend

BIRDOSWALD *(Banna)* ROMAN FORT

This fort sits on top of the escarpment over-looking the River Irthing, with splendid views over the valley. To the north the view is more restricted. A road led north from Birdoswald to the outpost fort at Bewcastle.

Most of the circuit of the walls and gates of Birdoswald are in the care of English Heritage; the fort and the surrounding land are owned by Cumbria County Council.

Birdoswald lies in the turf sector of Hadrian's Wall and the original fort here may have been of turf and timber, but if so, it was soon replaced in stone. Like the other forts, it was an addition to the Wall.

RIGHT: Reconstruction drawing of the granaries. There is no evidence for an upper floor (or door), though the size of the buildings does allow for such a possibility

BELOW: The demolished north granary was replaced by a timber hall rather larger than the granary. The pillars of the hall are marked by modern posts

EAST CUMBRIA COUNTRYSIDE PROJECT

47

TOUR OF BIRDOSWALD (Banna) ROMAN FORT

The **entrance** in the north wall leads into the **exhibition centre**. To the right lies the **north-west corner** of the fort; here the fort now sits free of Hadrian's Wall, which once abutted the corner. Inside the corner is a tower containing the remains of two ovens. In front of the former farmhouse lie the **west gate**, **granaries**, a

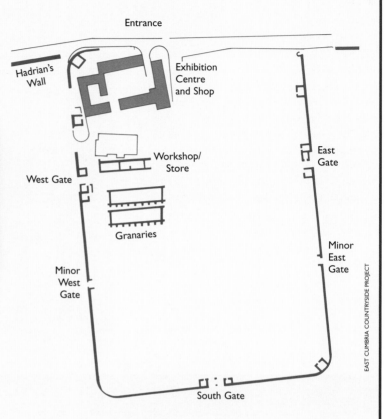

The outside face of the south tower of the west gate exhibits unusually fine masonry; the reason for this is not known

workshop or **store**, to the north of which was a hall or **basilica**. Cross the stile and turn right, heading for the **minor west gate**. The inner ditch of the fort survives as a faint hollow and can be traced round the south-west corner of the fort. A few paces from this corner is the edge of the Irthing escarpment.

Minor west gate at Birdoswald

The **south gate** is visible and along the **east wall** can be seen evidence of successive repairs. The **east gate** is one of the best preserved along the Wall and survives to the top of the pier. Evidence of long use is obvious in the renewal of the gate pivot stones and the modifications to the north tower. North of the gate is another interval tower.

The east gate of Birdoswald, with its twin entrances, still stands to the height of the first stone of the arch

It originally lay astride the turf wall, part of which was demolished to accommodate the fort. Later, when the turf wall was rebuilt in stone, the Wall line was moved north so that it met the northern corners of the fort instead of the towers of the main side gates. Birdoswald's garrison under Hadrian is not known, but from the early third century it was the home of the First Aelian Cohort of Dacians. This regiment was raised in what is now Romania and, although it will have subsequently recruited from Britain, it continued to display on its altars a symbol of its origin, the curved Dacian sword.

Recent excavations have demonstrated a vigorous occupation of the fort continuing to the very end of Roman Britain, and almost certainly beyond. A worn coin of the Emperor Theodosius I (388–95) was sealed by the collapsed roof of the north granary, over which was erected a large timber hall. This in turn was replaced by a second timber hall which is marked out by posts today. The very size of this building suggests that it was erected for a local chief. While the hall may not have survived the sixth century, the adjacent west gate of the fort continued in occupation well into the medieval period, perhaps even into the fifteenth century.

FINDS FROM BIRDOSWALD

Leather shoe

TULLIE HOUSE MUSEUM
& ART GALLERY, CARLISLE

An armpurse

TULLIE HOUSE MUSEUM & ART GALLERY, CARLISLE

Statue of Fortuna found in the commanding officer's bath house at Birdoswald

BELOW: Reconstruction of the west gate

EAST CUMBRIA COUNTRYSIDE PROJECT

TULLIE HOUSE MUSEUM & ART GALLERY, CARLISLE

Gold earrings. These would have been valuable possessions

A disc-headed pin

TULLIE HOUSE MUSEUM & ART GALLERY, CARLISLE

Bowness-on-Solway
CARLISLE
Birdoswald
Willowford Cawfields
Walltown
Vindolanda
Sewingshields Carrawburgh
Housesteads
Chesters
Brunton
Turret
Corbridge
Roman Town
Heddon-on-
the-Wall
NEWCASTLE
UPON TYNE
South Shields
Roman Fort
Wallsend

THE TURF WALL

ABOVE: This stone on the south face of the Wall between Harrow's Scar milecastle and Birdoswald fort records the building of a section of wall by the century of Terentius

FAR RIGHT, ABOVE: A model of a turret on the turf sector of the Wall

FAR RIGHT, BELOW: Turret 52a (Banks East)

ABOVE: A phallic symbol on the south face of the Wall between Harrow's Scar milecastle and Birdoswald fort. This represented good fortune and protection against evil

RIGHT: Hadrian's Wall running eastwards from Birdoswald to Harrow's Scar is the longest visible stretch of Wall rebuilt in stone

The whole of the western 30 miles (48 km) of Hadrian's Wall, from the crossing of the River Irthing at Harrow's Scar to Bowness-on-Solway, was originally built of turf. It was probably during Hadrian's reign that a start was made on rebuilding this section of the Wall in stone, and the work continued when Hadrian's Wall was reoccupied in the 160s. The first two Roman miles (3.2 km) west of the Irthing were replaced on a different line. West of Birdoswald, the remains of the turf wall can still be seen running behind the later stone wall.

East of Birdoswald, a complete one-third of a Roman mile of wall stretches to Harrow's Scar milecastle. To the north, the ditch is impressive and it is worth walking along the north side to the milecastle and back along the south. In the south face several building inscriptions and phallic symbols (to ward off evil spirits) can still be seen.

To the west of Birdoswald the remains lie beside the modern road. The first turret (49b) is a later (but still Hadrianic) stone wall turret, bonded in with the Wall. The next three visible turrets were earlier stone towers, built freestanding to receive the turf rampart on either side. On the rise to the east of the last visible turret, 52a (Banks East), lies a fragment of an earlier observation tower, Pike Hill. The troops posted here communicated back to the forts on the

Stanegate. A short, but tall, length of the Wall can be seen at Hare Hill; the facing stones were added in the nineteenth century. One mile along the road to the south-west, several Roman stones are on display in the undercroft at Lanercost Priory.

Sewingshields Carrawburgh
Housesteads
Willowford Cawfields   Chesters
Birdoswald   Brunton
                     Turret
Walltown Vindolanda
            Corbridge
            Roman Town

Heddon-on-   South Shields
the-Wall   Roman Fort
NEWCASTLE
UPON TYNE

wness-
Solway   Wallsend
aryport
CARLISLE

MARYPORT (*Alauna*) AND THE
SOLWAY FRONTIER

Hadrian's Wall ended at Bowness-on-Solway. Beyond here the coast was protected by forts, milefortlets and towers. Today, little is visible other than the fortlet at Swarthy Hill and the well-preserved earthworks of the fort at Maryport two miles (3 km) further south. The fort lies on private land, but may be viewed from the tower in the grounds of the adjacent museum.

The fort at Maryport is one of the largest on the frontier at 5.4 acres (2.3 hectares). It was probably built under Hadrian for the First Cohort of Spaniards, which was followed in the second century by the First Cohort of Dalmatians and the First Cohort of Baetasians, a regiment originally raised in the lower Rhineland. The names of the units based here in the third and fourth centuries are not known.

The museum at Maryport, the Senhouse Roman Museum, contains one of the oldest private collections in Britain, having been founded before 1599. It is remarkable for its altars, mostly dedicated to Jupiter, and the depictions of local Celtic gods. These cast a fascinating light on the religious activities of the Roman army.

LEFT: A horned god – a fertility god with roots deep in prehistory. Maryport was clearly a cult centre, as more depictions have been found of this god here than anywhere else in Britain

ABOVE: A short length of Stanwix fort wall in the Cumbria Hotel car park

LEFT: The earthworks of the fort at Maryport are clearly visible from the air. Each side contains a gate and beyond the wide ramparts lie two ditches. The fort is not open to the public but can be viewed from the adjacent museum, to the left on this photograph

© R BEWLEY

Twice a year, vows were fulfilled for the safety of the emperor over the last year, and undertaken for his wellbeing during the following year. (The appropriate sacrifice was an ox.) These ceremonies were undertaken on 3 January, two days after every unit in the army had renewed its oath of allegiance to the emperor, and on the anniversary of the emperor's accession. Altars dedicated on such occasions may have been erected in a special shrine to Jupiter situated north of the fort.

Maryport appears to possess an almost complete sequence of annual dedications erected by the First Cohort of Spaniards during the reign of Hadrian. These reveal that the average duration of command was three years. The commanders were drawn from Italy, Provence, *Noricum* (modern Austria), north Africa and possibly Spain. They moved on to posts in the Danubian provinces, Dacia (modern Romania) and Judaea.

LEFT: This altar was dedicated to Jupiter by Marcus Maenius Agrippa on behalf of the First Cohort of Spaniards. Agrippa, we know from his career inscription erected at Camerinum in Italy, was a friend of Hadrian. Agrippa was probably the first commander of the newly constructed fort at Maryport in about 123

ABOVE: The 'Serpent Stone' is a large phallic symbol; it takes its name from the serpent that runs up the entire length of one side. On the reverse is a human face framed by two snakes. The stone combines two important symbols: the phallus, a fertility symbol, and the human head, venerated by the Celts as being symbolic of divinity

BELOW: The milefortlet at Swarthy Hill looking west. This is one of a series of milefortlets and towers along the Cumbrian coast; most were abandoned during the second century